Overcoming Smallness:
Challenges and Opportunities for Small States in Global Affairs

OVERCOMING SMALLNESS:

Challenges & Opportunities For Small States In Global Affairs

Rory Miller & Fahad Al-Marri

Foreword By
H.E. Sheikha Alya Ahmed bin Saif Al-Thani

HAMAD BIN KHALIFA UNIVERSITY PRESS

Hamad Bin Khalifa University Press
P.O. Box 5825
Doha, Qatar

www.hbkupress.com

All rights reserved.

Cover photo: Alberto Andrei Rosu / Shutterstock.com

No part of this publication may be reproduced or transmitted in any form or by any means, electronic or mechanical, including photocopying, recording, or any information storage or retrieval system, without prior permission in writing from the publishers.

No responsibility for loss caused to any individual or organization acting on or refraining from action as a result of the material in this publication can be accepted by HBKU Press or the author.

The opinions expressed in this book do not necessarily reflect the opinion of the publisher.

First English edition in 2022
ISBN: 9789927155987

Printed in Beirut-Lebanon

Qatar National Library Cataloging-in-Publication (CIP)

Miller, Rory, 1971- author.

Overcoming smallness : challenges and opportunities for small states in global affairs / Rory Miller & Fahad Al-Marri ; forward by H.E. Sheikha Alya Ahmed Bin Saif Al-Thani. - First English edition. Doha, Qatar : Hamad Bin Khalifa University Press, 2022.

176 pages ; 24 cm

ISBN 978-992-715-598-7 (pbk)
ISBN 978-992-716-125-4 (hbk)

Includes bibliographical references (pages 165-175).

1. States, Small -- Case studies. 2. Qatar -- Politics and government -- 21st century. 3. Qatar -- Foreign relations -- 21st century. I. Al-Marri, Fahad, author. II. Title.

JC365 .M45 2022
320.1– dc 23   202228353973

Contents

ACKNOWLEDGEMENTS 9

FOREWORD 11

ABBREVIATIONS 15

CHAPTER 1
Small States, Foreign Policy,
and the International System 17

CHAPTER 2
Small States and Economic Development 37

CHAPTER 3
Small States and National Resources 59

CHAPTER 4
Small States as Autonomous Security Actors 81

CHAPTER 5
Small States, Alliances and Security 103

CHAPTER 6
The Blockade of Qatar: Small States,
Foreign Policy and Security Options 125

CHAPTER 7
The Blockade of Qatar: Small States,
Economic Development and National Resources 145

BIBLIOGRAPHY 165

*For our children: Erin, Maddy,
Bedour, Hussain, Tamim, Shaikha and Roda*

ACKNOWLEDGEMENTS

This book is intended to provide interested readers with an understanding of the role of small states on the regional level and across the international system, with a particular emphasis on the economic, security and institutional challenges and opportunities that they face in the contemporary era. This book is the result of an idea we had to co-teach a joint course at Georgetown University in Qatar on Small State Security in the International System. This innovative course combines classroom teaching with the regular and engaged participation of senior officials and national decision-makers who come together with our students in a Small State Dialogue to share their expertise.

We have welcomed the following distinguished guests so far to our Small State Dialogue (in order of appearance): H.E. Lolwah Rashid Al-Khater, Assistant Foreign Minister of the State of Qatar; H.E. Dr. Ibrahim Ibrahim, Former Economic Advisor at Amiri Diwan of the State of Qatar and Former Secretary-General of the General Secretariat for Development Planning of the State of Qatar; H.E. Dr. Khalid bin Mohamed Al-Attiyah, Deputy Prime Minister and Minister of State for Defense Affairs of the State of Qatar; Brigadier General. Nawaf bin Mubarak Al-Thani, Former Senior Defense Official and Defense Attaché of the State of Qatar to the United States of America, Mexico and Canada and Former Official Spokesperson for the Ministry of Defense of the State of Qatar; H.E. Sheikha Alya Ahmed bin Saif Al-Thani, Permanent Representative of the State of Qatar to the United Nations in New York; Mr. Yousuf bin Mohamed Al-Jaida, Chief Executive Officer, Qatar Financial Center; H.E. Sheikh Abdullah bin Saoud Al-Thani, Former Governor, Qatar Central Bank; H.E. Abdullah bin Hamad Al-Attiyah, Former Deputy Prime Minister and Minister of Energy & Industry of the State of Qatar; H.E. Sheikh Mohammed bin Abdulrahman bin Jassim Al-Thani, Deputy Prime Minister and Minister of Foreign Affairs of the

State of Qatar; H.E. Fahad bin Mohamed Al-Attiyah, Ambassador Ext. and Plen. of the State of Qatar to the United Kingdom; H.E. Dr. Mutlaq bin Majed Al-Qahtani, Special Envoy of the Minister of Foreign Affairs of the State of Qatar for Counterterrorism and Mediation in Conflict Resolution; H.E. Saad bin Mohammed Al-Rumaihi, Chairman of Qatar Press Center and Former Secretary for Follow-Up Affairs for the Amir of the State of Qatar; Major General. Abdullah bin Mohammed Al-Dosari, Chief of Intelligence and Security Authority of Qatar Armed Forces; H.E. Dr. Ahmed bin Mohammed Al-Muraikhi, Special Adviser to UN Secretary-General; H.E. Sumaya Baqavi, Deputy Chief of Mission & Counsellor (Political), of the Republic of Singapore to Qatar; Mr. Mansoor bin Ebrahim Al-Mahmoud, Chief Executive Officer, Qatar Investment Authority; and H.E. Saad bin Sherida Al-Kaabi, Minister of State for Energy Affairs of the State of Qatar, Deputy Chairman and President & CEO of QatarEnergy.

In all of their contributions, these senior officials have drawn on their wide-ranging practical experiences and their deep knowledge of relevant issues to consider the challenges and opportunities that small states in general, and Qatar in particular, encounter. These informed and informative talks have been very beneficial to our students who have had the opportunity to experience first-hand the ways that senior policy actors think about small state development and policy-making in domestic and international affairs. We are very grateful to all of our guests for the time they have invested in preparing and presenting their talks before our students. We are especially grateful to H.E. Sheikha Alya Ahmed bin Saif Al-Thani, Permanent Representative of the State of Qatar to the United Nations in New York, who agreed to write this book's foreword.

We would also like to thank all those students who have participated in this Dialogue with senior officials. In many ways this book is a result of all the hours we have spent discussing small states with them. Finally, we would like to thank our editors at HBKU Press for their generous support and encouragement for this project. This book has greatly benefited from their expert advice and recommendations.

Rory Miller and Fahad Al-Marri

FOREWORD

H.E. Sheikha Alya Ahmed bin Saif Al-Thani, Permanent Representative of the State of Qatar to the United Nations in New York

Today, small states comprise the majority of United Nations Member States. They are major players in multilateral diplomacy; the strongest advocates for inclusive multilateralism, global governance, and solidarity, which underpin the UN charter and 2030 Agenda for Sustainable Development.

As the Permanent Representative of the State of Qatar to the United Nations in New York, I have the opportunity to work with colleagues from many vibrant and dynamic small states on a daily basis. We are often at the forefront of tackling the world's most pressing issues from climate change and sustainability to conflict prevention and resolution. We are also among the most vocal champions in the fight against poverty, access to health and quality education, ending inequalities, and responding to climate change.

For instance, during this challenging time in history, as the COVID-19 pandemic continues, exacting a heavy toll on lives, societies, and economies in all regions of the world, small states have been at the forefront of global solidarity, working together to end the pandemic, calling for building back better and greener, and universal access to COVID-19 vaccines.

This underscores the point made in this book that states, irrespective of their size, can be highly effective actors, capable of adapting to new circumstances by initiating innovative approaches to problem-solving. Small states are very skilful at prioritizing the entire range of issues in the global agenda. Small states have served as key drafters, negotiators and thought leaders on a variety of issues, and have made remarkable contributions to global policy.

For instance, the State of Qatar, under the wise guidance and leadership of His Highness Sheikh Tamim bin Hamad Al-Thani, Amir of the State of Qatar, has assumed an active role within the international community, supporting international efforts to address climate change, sustainable development, humanitarian action, as well as initiatives to combat terrorism and maintain peace.

As an active UN Member State, the State of Qatar often brings together leaders in policy to discuss critical challenges facing our world, and promoting the interchange of ideas and discourse towards policy making and action-oriented recommendations.

Qatar believes in building alliances and finding solutions to conflicts through dialogue and mediation, while respecting the rights of sovereign nations. It has built a reputation as a mediator in regional disputes and has worked hard to promote regional and international security and sustaining peace. Recently, it has exerted considerable efforts to advance peace in Afghanistan. Doha became the hub for both international diplomatic action and humanitarian action in connection with Afghanistan. It has also played the leading role in facilitating the evacuation of over 60,000 foreign nationals and Afghans. Qatari technical teams have been working on partial repairs to Kabul Airport in order to allow and facilitate access of urgent humanitarian aid and movement of people.

An issue close to the heart of the Qatari people, are our international efforts to ensure that all children and youth have access to quality education, including those living in areas affected by crisis and conflict, and empowering our youth to take charge of their lives and make the world a better place for everyone.

Thanks to the efforts of the State of Qatar, ground-breaking United Nations General Assembly Resolutions have been adopted. Just to name a few: Resolution 62/139 which sets 2 April of each year as World Autism Day, a day to celebrate the countless ways that people with autism contribute to our families, our communities, and the world, and to shine a light on the systemic barriers people with autism face in their daily lives; landmark Resolution 64/290 calling on states to ensure the Right to

Education for affected populations in all phases of emergency situations; Resolution 74/275 establishing 9 September as the International Day to Protect Education from Attack, which sends a clear message regarding the importance of safeguarding schools as places of protection and safety for students and educators, and the need to keep education at the top of the public agenda; Resolution 75/274 establishing March 10 as the International Day of Women Judges, a recognition of the importance of women judges to the implementation of the rule of law, and fair and equal justice; and Resolution 71/248, establishing the International, Impartial and Independent Mechanism to assist in the investigation and prosecution of persons responsible for the most serious crimes under International Law committed in the Syrian Arab Republic since March 2011.

The State of Qatar is also leading international efforts to fight climate change and it has demonstrated global leadership by supporting the Least Developed Countries (LDCs) and Small Island Developing Countries (SIDS) achieve climate resilience and green growth in line with the UN's 2030 Agenda for Sustainable Development and the Paris Climate Agreement. These issues will be deliberated upon at the Fifth United Nations Conference on the Least Developed Countries (LDC5), on 5-9 March 2023, in Doha, which will be held at a critical time, and aims at building an ambitious new program for action for LDCs (Doha Programme of Action for LDCs for 2022–2031).

This book is particularly timely. It emerged from a course that the authors co-taught on small state security at Georgetown University in Qatar, in which I was one of several serving officials invited to address a class on how smallness, however understood, influences a state's actions and the relations between states in the areas of economics, trade, energy, finance, security and multilateral diplomacy. In my opinion, this is a valuable contribution made by this book because while rigorous and scholarly, it also considers smallness from the perspective of practitioners operating in a real-world context. This way, the authors tackle complex conceptual and analytical issues in a reader friendly way.

Moreover, its value also lies in the way that it repeatedly reminds us of how small states often drive forward key policies, advance mediation efforts, and promote fundamental human rights in crucial and effective ways. This underscores better than anything else the central argument of this excellent book: that small states are not only numerous but also key players in our complex and ever-changing world. Now, more than ever, this is a message that needs to be heard.

ABBREVIATIONS

ASEAN	Association of South East Asian States
ATP	Association of Tennis Professionals
AU	African Union
CENTCOM	US Central Command
CERD	Convention on the Elimination of All Forms of Racial. Discrimination
CIA	Central Intelligence Agency
COVID-19	Coronavirus
ESDP	European Security and Defence Policy
EU	European Union
FCMA	Treaty of Friendship, Cooperation and Mutual Assistance
FIFA	Fédération Internationale de Football Association
GCC	Gulf Cooperation Council
GDP	Gross Domestic Product
GHG	Global Greenhouse Gas
GNP	Gross National Product
GWOT	Global War on Terror
HDI	Human Development Index
ICC	International Criminal Court
ICJ	International Court of Justice
IMF	International Monetary Fund
IO	International Organization

IR	International Relations
LNG	Liquefied Natural Gas
MESA	Middle East Strategic Alliance
NATO	North Atlantic Treaty Organization
OECD	Organization of Economic Cooperation and Development
OSCE	Organization for Security and Cooperation in Europe
QF	Qatar Foundation
QIA	Qatar Investment Authority
QNV	Qatar National Vision
R&D	Research and Development
RO	Regional Organization
SARS	Severe acute respiratory syndrome
SIDS	Small Island Developing States
SWF	Sovereign Wealth Fund
UAE	United Arab Emirates
UN	United Nations
UNDP	United Nations Development Program
UNGA	United Nations General Assembly
WHO	World Health Organization
WTO	World Trade Organization

CHAPTER 1

Small States, Foreign Policy, and the International System

For over half a century, an entire sub-field of International Relations has been dedicated to the search for a definition of a small state. This exercise has included extensive discussions on the pros and cons of the suitability of various criteria and the limitations of existing definitions. There have also been various attempts at summarizing the debate and at formulating and reformulating the entire approach towards small state definitions. While there is no agreed definition of a small state or microstate, this does not stem from difficulties defining what a state is. Special small territories without political and legal sovereignty are normally not considered to be states. These include British Crown Dependencies, Chinese Special Administrative Regions, and the overseas territories of Australia, Denmark, France, The Netherlands, Norway, the United States and the United Kingdom.

The problem lies is defining what small or very small means. Maass distinguishes three broad categories of small state definitions that have been introduced and debated in the literature: quantitative, qualitative and auto-definitions.[1] He also notes that quantitative definitions are the most commonly used criteria for identifying small states.[2] These include a state's population size, though this measure is also widely regarded as a

---

1 Matthias Maass, "The Elusive Definition of the Small State," *International Politics* 46, no. 1 (2009): 65–83.
2 Aart Kraay and William Easterly, "Small States, Small Problems?," *Policy Research Working Papers* (World Bank, Washington D.C, 1999). https://elibrary.worldbank.org/doi/abs/10.1596/1813-9450-2139.

convenient short-hand for a composite of different measures of population rather than a single, independent criterion.[1]

Notably, over the decades, scholars have tended to prioritize certain quantitative measures over others. Karl Deutsch, for example, argued that GNP is the most important single quantitative measure of state size.[2] East in the 1970s, and Ólafsson much more recently, argued in favor of a wider set of criteria, respectively: population size, size of territory and GNP, military strength and total land area.[3] Others have challenged these perspectives, and have argued that territorial area is "irrelevant" to the question of size[4] and that GNP is not the most important single quantitative measure.[5]

Despite such disagreements, quantitative approaches would provide many advantages for the field of small state research if there existed a unified index or criterion that could be adopted. As this is not the case, there are a number of problems with quantitative definitions. They demand arbitrary cut-off points in time and the significance of certain numbers change over time—a population of five million in the 1950s, for example, might represent something very different in terms of standing and influence than a population of five million in the twenty-first century.

In the absence of a rigorous quantitative framework for assessing "smallness," Bailes, Thayer and Thorhallsson have argued against

---

1 Commonwealth Secretariat, *Vulnerability: Small States in the Global Society. Report of a Commonwealth Consultative Group* (Commonwealth Secretariat, 1985), 8, https://www.amazon.com/Vulnerability-Small-States-Global-Society/dp/0850922801.

2 Karl W. Deutsch, *The Analysis of International Relations* (Englewood Cliffs, NJ: Prentice-Hall, Inc., 1968).

3 M. East, "Size and Foreign Policy Behavior: A Test of Two Models," *World Politics* 25, no. 4 (1973): 556–576; Björn G. Ólafsson, *Small States in Global System: Analysis and Illustrations from the Case of Iceland* (Ashgate: Aldershot, 1998), 8–10.

4 Franz Von Däniken, "Is the Notion of Small State Still Relevant?," in *Small States Inside and Outside the European Union: Interests and Policies*, ed. L. Goetschel (Boston, MA: Springer, 1998), 43–48.

5 Peter R. Baehr, "Small States: A Tool for Analysis?," *World Politics* 27, no. 3 (1975): 456–466.

"one-dimensional quantitative measures," and instead have made the case for recognizing the "complexities inherent in categorization." On that basis, they have called for an approach centered on "diversity" that includes a significant qualitative component.[1]

Unlike quantitative attempts at formulating definitions of small states, qualitative ones are not primarily intended to be based on a rational cut-off point of indices but on a combination of criteria that are often a product of one's intuition. Understandably, this "I know a small state when I see one" approach is quite widely used, but its vagueness and subjectivity also raises its own set of problems. An auto-definition attempts to address the limitations of both quantitative and qualitative approaches. It considers how a state self-identifies as the decisive factor in labelling it small or not. Finland, as Browning has shown,[2] is an example of one small state that has engaged in a shifting discourse over its own identity regarding its smallness, peripherality, weakness and smartness.

The problem with adopting an auto-definition is that just because a country self-identifies as a small state does not mean that it is accurate or appropriate for it to do so or that others will agree to recognize it as such. South Korea, for example, self-identifies, in different contexts, as small but in 2018 it had the fourth largest economy in Asia and the twelfth largest in the world.[3] This raises another point. Countries may have a political interest in being defined as small as part of a soft or smart power international strategy. Self-defining as small may also appeal to states as a way for them to qualify for certain concessions and advantages in their various bilateral or multilateral relationships. These can include eligibility

---

1 Alyson J. K. Bailes, Bradley A. Thayer and Baldur Thorhallsson, "Alliance Theory and Alliance "Shelter": The Complexities of Small State Alliance Behaviour," *Third World Thematics: A TWQ Journal 1*, no. 1 (2016): 9–26.
2 Christopher Browning, "Small, Smart and Salient? Rethinking Identity in the Small States Literature," *Cambridge Review of International Affairs* 19, no. 4 (2006): 669–684.
3 "South Korea's 2018 GDP Growth Slows To 6-yr Low, Trade Woes Dim Outlook," *Nikkei Asian Review*, January 22, 2019 (Accessed February 15, 2020) https://asia.nikkei.com/Economy/South-Korea-s-2018-GDP-growth-slows-to-6-yr-low-trade-woes-dim-outlook.

for aid or technology transfer that is specifically reserved for small countries or reduced membership fees or fewer responsibilities and duties in International Organizations (IOs).

The definitional challenge faced by IOs is interesting in this context. A major report issued by the Commonwealth Secretariat and the World Bank in 2000 acknowledged the difficulty of reaching consensus on what a small state is. Drawing on its findings, this report made the case that "no definition, whether it be population, geographical size or Gross Domestic Product (GDP), is likely to be fully satisfactory."[1] This is due to the fact that all small states are unique in terms of their own histories and cultures, geographies and natural resources, and levels of development.

A lack of definitional clarity can also appeal to IOs with numerous member states due to a "political calculation that any definition would be contested by some countries."[2] While the World Bank does define a small state as one with a small population, limited human capital, and a confined land area,[3] other IOs prefer to either avoid the issue altogether or provide general or even contradictory definitions. The Commonwealth, for example, considers countries with populations of less than 1.5 million as small but also includes countries with bigger populations (such as Jamaica at 2.8 million or Lesotho at 2.3 million) in the same category if they share other characteristics of smallness. In consequence, thirty-one of the Commonwealth's fifty-three members are considered by the organization to be small states.

Other IOs avoid such confusion by refusing to participate completely in the debate on small state definitions. As a 2002 World Trade Organization (WTO) report put it, any list of small states would "include countries that are heterogeneous in some respects and can be easily

---

1   Commonwealth Secretariat/World Bank Joint Task Force, *Small States: Meeting Challenges in the Global Economy* (Washington, DC, World Bank, 2000). http://documents.worldbank.org/curated/en/267231468763824990/Small-states-meeting-challenges-in-the-global-economy.
2   Paul Sutton, "The Concept of Small States in the International Political Economy," *The Round Table: The Commonwealth Journal of International Affairs* 100, no. 413 (2011):141–153.
3   The World Bank, *The World Bank in Small States*. https://www.worldbank.org/en/country/smallstates.

criticized, since the analysis of common characteristics turns out to be difficult."[1] In recognition of this, the previous year the WTO established a "Work Programme on Small Economies."[2] Over the next several years it focused its research, analysis and policy proposals on what it termed the "small vulnerable economy," rather than the small state. Interestingly, this refocusing on the political economies of smaller state actors did not solve the definitional problem because, as Sutton has noted, the WTO also chose not to provide a definition of a "small vulnerable economy." In part, this can again be explained by the fact that no two small states share the same vulnerabilities or challenges, something that serves to further differentiate them from one another. But it is also due to political sensitivities and concerns over the implications of creating a special subcategory inside the WTO that might raise protests or necessitate special treatment for some members on the basis of size.[3]

Many scholars still consider the search for a definition of a small state to be important. This is evidenced by the continued existence of a large sub-field of International Relations scholars working on the broad theme of small states. Among this group, those who are offended by definitional ambiguity argue that its absence is the key reason why small state research is fragmented and still relatively "overlooked" in the wider discipline of International Relations.[4] As Long put it in 2017, "The lack of clarity over how to understand and delimit the central object of study has hindered theory building, complicated comparison and cumulation, and obfuscated the conversation with International Relations theory more broadly."[5]

The absence of a precise small state definition is not problematic for all scholars. Some argue instead that it is completely legitimate to be

---

1 World Trade Organization, *Small Economies: A Literature Review*, Committee on Trade and Development, (2002), 2-3. WT/COMTD/SE/W/4.
2 World Trade Organization, Work Programme on Small Economies, https://www.wto.org/english/tratop_e/devel_e/dev_wkprog_smalleco_e.htm.
3 Sutton, "The Concept of Small States in the International Political Economy," 148.
4 Ibid.
5 Tom Long, "It's Not The Size, It's The Relationship: From 'Small States' to Asymmetry," *International Politics* 54, no. 2, (2017):144–160.

"imprecise" in terms of quantifiable data.[1] One practical consequence of this embrace of ambiguity is that it allows for the drawing up of definitions on a case by case basis. This is in line with a growing body of work that rejects the notion of a unitary category of small states or at least tends to view such traditional thinking critically. Browning has argued that "pertinent identity narratives" that include "smart" or "innovative" national characteristics are increasingly important considerations compared to size.

Closely connected to this argument is the view that the big-state-small-state dichotomy has been superseded by a core-periphery approach. In these terms, the global economy is characterized by a structured relationship between different economic centers of power. These actors use various instruments of national power—economic, military and political—to extract economic surpluses from subordinate peripheral actors, who may or may not be small states.[2]

The argument made by Gigleux and others that it is unproductive to link size to patterns of small state behavior in international affairs has also gained significant traction in recent times.[3] This seems to be especially true in an era of globalization, in which it is increasingly accepted that neither demography nor territorial size can satisfactorily explain political behavior or national power capabilities. Instead, the power and influence of small states in relation to more materially strong actors or threats can be achieved through and understood in terms of multiple channels, most notably the skilled mobilization of non-material ideational and identity factors.[4]

Given the difficulty of achieving an agreement on a small state definition

---

1   Maass, "The Elusive Definition of the Small State," 76.
2   Browning, "Small, Smart and Salient? Rethinking Identity in the Small States Literature," 678.
3   Victor Gigleux, "Explaining the Diversity of Small States' Foreign Policies Through Role Theory," *Third World Thematics: A TWQ Journal* 1, no. 1 (2016): 27–45.
4   Silvia Colombo, "Foreign Policy Activism in Saudi Arabia And Oman. Diverging Narratives And Stances Towards The Syrian and Yemeni Conflicts," *The International Spectator: Italian Journal of International Affairs* 52, no. 2 (2017): 54–70.

or even on whether having one matters, one option for researchers is to abandon the search for consensus and instead allow, as mentioned above, for auto-definition by states themselves or for qualitative definitions by researchers on the basis of their own preferred criteria. Väyrynen, for example, measures smallness somewhat arbitrarily in these terms on the basis of the nature of state behavior, and the distinct interests of the actor in question in relation to larger powers.[1] One advantage of this approach is that it can contribute to a more accurate assessment of how different aspects of smallness—including, but not limited to, traditional measures of population size, military strength, natural resources—have different levels of relevance in different contexts: including international relations and diplomacy, trade and investment, domestic development and institution building.

In the absence of a single small state category one can also look to distinguish between several types of small states. One can do this by developing, in line with Väyrynen's approach, a common understanding of the nature of relationships between different actors rather than considering size in itself as the key factor. A small state can, for example, also be medium or even large in relation to an even smaller one and, as such, whether a particular state is small can be defined relationally.[2] To take one example from the European context—Sweden, Belgium and Greece are medium-sized compared to Malta and Luxembourg. However, all five are dwarfed economically and militarily by the big member states—France, Germany and, prior to Brexit, the United Kingdom. This fact explains, to some extent at least, the different levels of influence and leadership of these members within the European Union (EU) policy making process—an issue that will be addressed later in this book.

It is also possible to categorize smallness in terms of certain specific

---

1   R. Väyrynen, "On the Definition and Measurement of Small Power Status," *Cooperation and Conflict: Journal of the Nordic International Studies Association* 2, (1971): 91–102; Olle Krantz, "Small European Countries In Economic Internationalisation: An Economic Historical Perspective," Umeå Papers in Economic History, no. 26 (2006).
2   Anders Wivel and Kajsa Ji Noe Oest, "Security, Profit or Shadow of The Past? Explaining the Security Strategies of Microstates," *Cambridge Review of International Affairs* 23, no. 3 (2010): 429–453.

vulnerabilities. This is in line with the WTO's focus on small vulnerable economies and the Commonwealth's focus on vulnerable island states, which make up a significant percentage of the Commonwealth's members. This approach does require further clarification in the scholarship—notably in relation to assessing which characteristics of smallness have the most negative consequences across a range of events. Nevertheless, it still offers a useful way to conceptualize and better understand small states. It certainly serves an important function in underscoring the point that smallness is likely to be most relevant in terms of impact and consequences in some areas of endeavor more than in others (security or trade), or in response to specific kinds of military, financial or environmental shocks.

Smallness, for example, may magnify the negative impact of natural disasters like hurricanes, droughts and volcanic eruptions. This is a particularly important observation because three out of four developing small states are either islands, widely dispersed multi-island states, or landlocked territories. In economic terms, this also raises the obvious challenge of having a small domestic market isolated from larger markets, something that can impact on competitiveness, efficiency, innovativeness and resilience. It can also make small states economically dependent on larger neighbors, especially in key sectors. Ireland exports around 49 percent of its beef and 82 percent of its milk to the United Kingdom, something that has raised concerns in both sectors in the post-Brexit era.[1] Similarly, when the blockade of Qatar began in the summer of 2017, the country was highly dependent on food products from Saudi Arabia. The shared Salwa border also served as a key transit hub for multiple countries importing into Qatar a variety of food groups such as poultry eggs, dairy milk, salad crops, fruits, and oils.[2]

As Cooper and Moami have noted, the Euro-Zone financial crisis

---

[1] "As Brexit Looms, How Dependent is Ireland on British Trade?," *DW*, February 4, 2019 (Accessed June 20, 2020) https://www.dw.com/en/fact-check-as-brexit-looms-how-dependent-is-ireland-on-british-trade/a-47322998.

[2] Tareq Al-Ansari, "Food Security: The Case of Qatar," in *The Gulf Crisis: The View from Qatar*, ed. Rory Miller (Doha: Hamad bin Khalifa University Press, 2018), 28–38.

highlighted the real financial and economic vulnerabilities faced by several small European states inside and outside of the EU: Cyprus, Greece, Ireland, Portugal, Estonia, Lithuania, Latvia and Iceland, to name some of the worst affected.[1] More generally, states with small populations can also find capacity building in both the public and private sectors particularly challenging, and can find it more difficult to diversify their local economies than larger states, especially when a single commodity is the dominant source of revenues.

Small States, Foreign Policy and the International System

During the nineteenth and twentieth centuries, smaller state actors found it extremely difficult to shape, or even contribute to, decision-making on war, peace and trade in the international system.[2] Indeed, long after the end of the Second World War, perceptions of size continued to play an important role in determining attitudes over whether a territorial unit was fit for statehood. This view was reflected in the International Relations scholarship during the 1960s and 1970s, at a time of rapid decolonization and at the height of a superpower Cold War between the Soviet Union and the United States. A group of influential thinkers, including Maurice East, David Vital, Robert Rothstein, Robert Keohane and Robert Jervis, held contradictory views on how best to define a small state, but they all agreed on three general principles as they related to the status of small states in the international system.

First, these eminent scholars made the case that small states are far more sensitive than larger powers to changes in the external environment and that those changes will have a greater impact on small states because, as Jervis argued, they lack a "margin of time and error" when responding

---

1 Andrew F. Cooper and Bessma Momani, "Qatar and Expanded Contours of Small State Diplomacy," *The International Spectator: Italian Journal of International Affairs* 46, no. 3 (2011): 113–128.

2 Graham Ross, *The Great Powers and the Decline of the European States System* (London: Longman, 1983), 39–41; Matthias Maass, "Small Enough to Fail: The Structural Irrelevance of the Small State as Cause of its Elimination and Proliferation since Westphalia," *Cambridge Review of International Affairs* 29, no. 4 (2016): 1303–1323.

to external exigencies.[1] The ease with which 100,000 Iraqi troops and 700 tanks entered and occupied Kuwait in August 1990 is an excellent example of this vulnerability. Once the invasion began, the Kuwaiti air force remained operational for twenty-four hours and army units located in the area around the Amir's palace did manage to hold off invading Iraqi troops for a couple of hours. Otherwise, Iraqi forces faced little resistance elsewhere as they overran the country.

These scholars also argued that small states clearly understand the difficult predicament that they face or, as Vital famously put it, "Weakness [is the] most common, natural and pervasive view of *self* in the small state."[2] This understanding of their own vulnerabilities, and especially their limited capacity to move beyond foreign engagement that is both reactive and involuntary, causes small states to be more preoccupied than bigger actors with immediate security concerns and their own survival. It also forces them to acknowledge, in the words of Rothstein and Keohane respectively, that they "cannot obtain security primarily by use of [their] own capabilities" and "can never, acting alone or in a small group, make a significant impact on the system."[3] In recognition of this, chapter 5 of this book will examine the ways that small states look to join security alliances and regional organizations (ROs) in their quest for security.

The introduction of many of these arguments in the literature coincided with a wide-ranging and passionate debate at the United Nations (UN) during the late 1960s and 1970s over whether it was proper and correct to classify newly independent small state actors, including micro-states with tiny populations, as sovereign states in the eyes of international law, and whether they would be able to fulfil the obligations of UN membership on entry.

---

1 Robert Jervis, "Cooperation Under the Security Dilemma," *World Politics* 30, no.2, (1978): 167–214; James N. Rosenau, *Turbulence in World Politics: A Theory of Change and Continuity* (New Jersey: Princeton University Press, 1990).
2 David Vital, *The Inequality of Small States* (Oxford: Clarendon Press, 1967), 33.
3 Robert L. Rothstein, *Alliances and Small Powers* (New York: Columbia University Press, 1968), 34–6;
Robert Keohane, "Lilliputians' Dilemmas: Small States in International Politics," *International Organization* 23, no. 2 (1969): 291–310.

Another major concern revolved around whether this growing constituency of smaller sovereign actors might pool their voting rights at the UN, in the process distorting the bipolar international system and undermining the Cold War balance of power between East and West.[1] Interestingly, research undertaken at this time on how states with small populations actually voted at the UN showed that they tended to vote together on colonial and economic issues rather than on social or cultural issues, but that size alone was a not sufficient way to differentiate the voting patterns of small states.[2]

Over subsequent decades, and despite the ongoing failure of scholars to develop an agreed definition of what constitutes a small state, the attitudes of policy-makers toward their viability improved as those small states that had joined the UN in the 1960s and 1970s developed, for the most part, into fully-functioning and productive members of the international community. As Hong has shown, in the early 1990s, in the years immediately following the end of the Cold War, there was real optimism that small states working together could bring about systematic change at the UN, including the reorganization and reform of the UN Security Council, and a rebalancing of the relationship between the General Assembly and the Security Council.[3]

In part, these changing views were due to the rising relevance of international organizations (IOs) including regional organizations (ROs) like the EU, African Union (AU), Association of South East Asian States (ASEAN) and the Gulf Cooperation Council (GCC). These institutions, as shall be examined in chapter 5, are structured in ways that in certain circumstances can provide smaller members with more leverage,

---

[1] W. L. Harris, "Microstates in the United Nations: A Broader Purpose," *Columbia Journal of Transnational Law* 9, (1970): 23-53; M. H. Mendelson, "Diminutive States in the United Nations," *International and Comparative Law Quarterly* 21 (1972): 609–630; M. M. Gunter, "What Happened to the United Nations Ministate Problem?," *American Journal of International Law* 71, (1977): 110–124.

[2] J. R. Harbert, "The Behavior of the Ministates in the United Nations, 1971–1972," *International Organization* 30, (1976): 109–127.

[3] M. Hong, "Small States in the United Nations," *International Social Science Journal* 47, no. 2 (1995): 277–287.

legitimacy, and the opportunity to bring about change that they would otherwise not have.

Nevertheless, in the decades since scholars like Jervis, Vital, and Rothstein, among others, made their own influential arguments over the inherent weakness of small states, it is still widely held, for example, that small states in the contemporary era find it difficult to assert their own interests in external affairs and that the most striking characteristic, and consequence, of smallness on the international stage remains vulnerability rather than power.[1]

Feldman, Papadakis and Starr, Thorhallsson, and many others, have demonstrated how smallness (however defined) is consistently a variable in distinguishing differences in foreign policy behavior and an important factor in determining the external influence of states.[2] Similarly, at the policy-level, the view remains that size is still a major determining factor of state behavior, especially outside of international and regional organizations, and that the participation of states outside of their own borders will be dictated by the size of their surplus capabilities.[3]

Size and surplus capabilities may remain major determining factors of state behavior, and the external environment will often define and constrain state action. At the same time, it is necessary to have a more nuanced view of the role of small states in the international system in terms of their power and influence. A state's perception of its own environment and its willingness to take particular courses of action, independent of size, are

---

1   Anthony Payne, "Small States in the Global Politics of Development," *The Round Table: The Commonwealth Journal of International Affairs* 93, no.376, (2004): 623–635.

2   Miriam Fendius Elman, "The Foreign Policies of Small States: Challenging Neorealism in its Own Backyard," *British Journal of Political Science* 25, no. 2 (1995): 171–217; M. Papadakis and H. Starr, "Opportunity, Willingness, and Small States: The Relationship Between Environment and Foreign Policy," in *New Directions in the Study of Foreign Policy*, eds. C. F. Hermann, C. W. Kegley, J. Rosenau (Boston: Allen & Unwin, 1987), 409–432; B. Thorhallsson, *The Role of Small States in the European Union* (Burlington, VT: Ashgate Publishing Company, 2000).

3   G. L. Reid, *The Impact of Very Small Size on the International Relations Behavior of Microstates* (London: Sage, 1974).

important drivers of policies and engagement.[1] Nor is it any longer the case that there exists a consensus that small states have no capacity for developing influence in foreign affairs, even if they are "political dwarfs."[2] Instead, it is now considered possible for small states to overcome size-related difficulties in the foreign policy sphere in ways that make it incorrect to always, or even regularly, equate smallness with weakness. On the contrary, some small states have successfully used or even transformed their smallness into strength in the international arena.

In line with the fact that small and geographically vulnerable does not have to mean permanently weak, many recent case studies have demonstrated that small states have more influence in the regional and international systems than was traditionally assumed. Ólafsson's analysis of the Icelandic model has shown that while, in objective terms, small states are suboptimal from the point of view of security and may also be suboptimal as political and economic units on the international level, there are "no serious disadvantages resulting from the small size of states in the global system."[3]

This however must be clarified. Even if one accepts that in practical or analytical terms small states have the power to conduct an independent foreign policy, it does not mean that it is also the case that they can have a significant impact on the structure of the international system itself.[4] They remain, as Keohane has termed it, "system-ineffectual" in contrast with the "system-determining" and "system-influencing" capacity of larger and more powerful states.[5] In other words, small states can have some power in international politics and the foreign policy realm, and their preferences may be heard, but their voices cannot necessarily determine international decision-making.

This is an important observation that may help us think about the limits of the foreign policy power of small states. Alternatively, one can

---

1   Papadakis and Starr, "Opportunity, Willingness, and Small States," 415–17.
2   Diana Panke, "Small States in EU Negotiations: Political Dwarfs or Power-Brokers?," *Cooperation and Conflict* 46, no.2, (2011):123–143.
3   Ólafsson, *Small States in Global System*, 4, 62, 153.
4   Maass, "Small Enough to Fail,", 1310.
5   Keohane, *Lilliputians' Dilemmas: Small States in International Politics*, 291–310.

argue that small states were historically inconsequential and irrelevant but that in today's world they are no longer irrelevant to the system and, under the right circumstances, can have as much impact on its structure as larger actors. Those who support this latter view place significant importance in the ways that small states use soft power.[1] This describes a concept of liberal power based around persuasion rather than coercion. It is a function of one actor's admiration for the values, culture and achievements of another. Adherents of soft power argue that as the appeal and role of hard power diminishes in the international system, such "attraction," as Joseph Nye has termed it, becomes increasingly important.

In terms of thinking about other forms of non-traditional or alternative power available to small states, Browning used Finland as a case study to show that it is possible to present smallness positively in the construction of state identities. This, he argues, can open the way for greater small state action in foreign policy and can also allow smallness to be replaced by the marker of being smart and innovative.[2] Some small states may, for example, possess certain skills among their human resources that are disproportionate to their physical size, including intellectual capital and visionary leaders. These can serve as forms of "compensatory symbolic power."[3] Chong has argued that small states can convert other non-typical sources of power including adaptability, creativity and moral capital into "instruments of virtual enlargement" which provide the opportunity for their "attempts to enlarge their importance to the international community."[4]

Though one can take issue with some of the conceptual underpinnings of these arguments by Chong and others, they do illuminate some of the options that small states have for converting their intangible, anomalous

---

1 G. John Ikenberry, "Review of Joseph S. Nye, Jr.: Soft Power: The Means to Success in World Politics," *Foreign Affairs* 83, no. 2 (May/June 2004):136–37.
2 Browning, "Small, Smart and Salient?," 669–684.
3 Alan Chong, "Small State Soft Power Strategies: Virtual Enlargement in the Cases of the Vatican City State and Singapore," *Cambridge Review of International Affairs* 23, no. 3 (2010): 383–405; Commonwealth Advisory Group, *A Future for Small States: Overcoming Vulnerability* (London: Commonwealth Secretariat, 1997), 177.
4 Chong, "Small State Soft Power Strategies," 386.

power into tangible influence. This process can, for example, be applied by small states in the ways they deal with economics, governance, and diplomacy. This was very evident during the WTO's Doha Round in the early 2000s, when smaller members of the organization mobilized support for their arguments on trade in terms of international values on development and in moral language that, in turn, successfully led to support for their preferred positions.[1] Another example, in the realm of diplomacy and statecraft, is the way that small states can take advantage of the widespread, though not necessarily accurate, equation of their lack of hard power capabilities with a commitment to peace and harmony in international affairs.[2]

Such perceptions can be manipulated by small states engaged in pro-actively developing "consciously constructed"[3] reputations as "good international citizens."[4] This is especially the case if the leaders of the small states in question understand and embrace the widely-held views of the roles expected of them at the national, regional or international levels.[5] The small Scandinavian states, including Finland, Norway and Sweden, are often presented as leading examples of how small states build on widely-held (self-)perceptions to engage in norm entrepreneurship in international affairs.[6] Notably, they have taken advantage of their remote geographic location, their unique domestic institutions, and in the case of Sweden and Finland, their neutrality, to develop their global reputation as trustworthy international actors.

---

1   Donna Lee and Nicola J. Smith, "Small State Discourses in the International Political Economy," *Third World Quarterly* 31, no. 7 (2010): 1091–1105, 1100–1.
2   Chong, "Small State Soft Power Strategies," 386.
3   C. Ingebritsen, "Norm Entrepreneurs: Scandinavia's Role in World Politics," *Cooperation and Conflict* 37, no. 1 (2002): 11–23.
4   Ken Ross, "The Commonwealth: A Leader for the World's Small States?," *The Round Table: The Commonwealth Journal of International Affairs* 86, no. 343 (1997): 411–419.
5   Väyrynen, "On the Definition and Measurement of Small Power Status," 91–102.
6   Annika Bjorkdahl, "Ideas and Norms in Swedish Peace Policy," *Swiss Political Science Review* 19, no. 3 (2013): 322–337; C. Ingebritsen, "Norm Entrepreneurs: Scandinavia's Role in World Politics," 11–23.

Long distinguishes three types of power that can be exercised by small states, like those in Scandinavia, in order to increase their influence in international affairs: intrinsic, derivative, and collective. His important conceptual contribution draws on Robert A. Dahl's earlier work, which categorized power in international affairs in terms of base, means, and scope. The base, Dahl argued, represented a state's power resources that could be exploited in ways that influence the behavior of another actor in the international system; the means referred to how the state utilizes its power resources (its base) through "threats and promises"; and the scope related to the range of responses that the actor can achieve on any given issue.[1]

In these terms, Long argues that each of his three categories of small state power—intrinsic, derivative, and collective—can be viewed as having different bases, which in turn translates into different means. This is because a small state or, at least in dyadic terms, the smaller state of two given actors, has relatively scarce international coercive capabilities. As such, it will prioritize and focus on a particular form of power that matches the bases it has available to achieve its goals through the application of certain means.

In a post-Dahlian sense, though small states lack many of the normal categories of capabilities, they may possess particular forms of intrinsic power.[2] If this is the case, then potential bases of power can become real in specific contexts when they are applied correctly. Oil is a good example. It is not power *per se* and can even bring with it the dreaded "resource curse"[3] (also known as the "paradox of plenty"), but if employed correctly in the right context, it can be very powerful. During the oil crisis of the mid-1970s, then US Secretary of State Henry Kissinger, addressed the rising power of the Arab Gulf oil-kingdoms, all of whom had previously had little political, military or economic influence even on the regional level. "Never before," Kissinger recalled, "had nations so weak

---

1 Robert A. Dahl, "The Concept of Power," *Behavioral Science* 2, no. 3 (1957): 201–215.
2 Long, "Small States, Great Power?," 194–195.
3 See Michael L. Ross, *The Oil Curse: How Petroleum Wealth Shapes the Development of Nations* (Princeton, New Jersey: Princeton University Press, 2013).

militarily—and in some cases politically—been able to impose such strains on the international system."[1]

Derivative power refers to a situation in which states are able to derive power by convincing larger states to take actions that boost their interests. One excellent recent example is former Israeli Prime Minister Benjamin Netanyahu's discussion of his country's efforts to influence Washington on the Iranian threat in an interview in the *New York Times*. "If it is possible to recruit the most powerful country in the world onto our side, why should we fight alone?" he asked, before adding "If I can harness a world power against Iran … why not?"

As this quote demonstrates, derivative power, which Keohane described as "the big influence of small allies,"[2] can be quite narrow in focus—in the above case, for example, it is only related to Israel's influence over the US on one regional security issue. Nonetheless, derivative power is likely to appeal to states that lack their own material capabilities but have a good relationship and share common interests with a major power. Handel, who argued that "the diplomatic art of the weak states is to obtain, commit, and manipulate, as far as possible, the power of other more powerful states in their own interests,"[3] considered this form of power to be the most important facet of a small state's strength.

If the fundamental base of derivative power is the relationship between the small state and a major power, then the fundamental base of collective power is the relationship between a small state and associated non-great powers, including regional middle powers and other small states. For this reason, small states, as East noted almost half a century ago, are inclined to initiate more joint behavior than larger states and the targets of their actions tend to be groups of states or intergovernmental organizations.[4] One advantage for small states in joining and building-up such institutions

---

1   Henry Kissinger, *Years of Renewal* (London: Phoenix Press,1989), 667.
2   Robert O. Keohane, "The Big Influence of Small Allies," *Foreign Policy* 2, (Spring 1971): 161–182.
3   Michael Handel, *Weak States in the International System* (London: Frank Cass, 1981), 257.
4   M. East, "Size and Foreign Policy Behavior: A Test of Two Models," *World Politics* 25, no. 4 (1973): 556–576.

is that it enables them to "minimize the costs,"[1] political as well as economic, of conducting foreign policy.

Participating in collective action via IOs, including ROs, can also provide small states with a say in the organization's decision-making processes.[2] By committing to play by the institution's rules, and by using the institution's internal mechanisms, the small state can facilitate the formulation of normative policies and promote its own priority national interests.[3] One example is the victory of Antigua and Barbuda over the United States inside the WTO in 2003, when the tiny archipelago was awarded US$21 million annually as compensation for the US excluding it from its massively lucrative gambling market.[4] Another is the success of some small island states in influencing international approaches to the climate change debate inside the UN and other multilateral fora. Notably, the Maldives government gained widespread media attention when its cabinet chose to hold a meeting underwater to highlight the need for further global cuts in carbon emissions.

Even if much of the recent research supports the view that small states can be influential foreign policy actors, this conclusion is mainly based on alternative conceptualizations of power, such as soft power, or is a consequence of the adoption of a unit-level analysis rather than a systemic analysis whereby the estimate of small state power focuses on a limited number of issues or characteristics rather than the more global whole. Indeed, while Antigua and Barbuda won an impressive victory over the

---

1 Iver B. Neumann and Sieglinde Gstöhl, "Introduction," in *Small States in International Relations*, eds. Christine Ingebritsen, Iver B. Neumann, Sieglinde Gstöhl, and Jessica Beyer (Seattle: University of Washington Press, 2006), 12.
2 Diana Panke, "Dwarfs in International Negotiations: How Small States Make their Voices Heard," *Cambridge Review of International Affairs* 25, no. 3 (2012): 313–328.
3 Mika Aaltola, Joonas Sipilä, and Valtteri Vuorisalo, "Securing Global Commons: A Small State Perspective," The Finnish Institute of International Affairs, Working Paper 71, June, 2011.
4 "DS285: United States—Measures Affecting the Cross-Border Supply of Gambling and Betting Services," World Trade Organization, December 3, 2020, https://www.wto.org/english/tratop_e/dispu_e/cases_e/ds285_e.htm.

United States inside the WTO, their very victory also raised a number of potential negative consequences for the tiny island states. As one trade expert put it, "If Antigua chooses to do so, it may set a precedent that provides small countries with useful leverage in trade disputes; but the difficulties of implementation and the harm done to Antigua's reputation might overwhelm and outlast the economic benefits."[1]

"One of the asymmetries of history," wrote Kissinger of Singapore's patriarch Lee Kuan Yew, "is the lack of correspondence between the abilities of some leaders and the power of their countries." President Richard Nixon spoke in even more flattering terms than his secretary of state about the founding father of Singapore. He speculated that had Lee lived in another time and another place, he might have "attained the world stature of a Churchill, a Disraeli, or a Gladstone."[2] These acknowledgements of Lee's talent by the two key Western decision-makers of the age underscore one final point. Alternative conceptualizations of power, such as visionary leadership in the case of Lee, may be of huge value for a small state in overcoming smallness. However, it is no less the case that such alternative forms of power can also be limited in their impact more broadly. When they are, it is smallness, however conceived, that has been, and remains, the most likely reason.

---

[1] Isaac Wohl, "The Antigua-United States Online Gambling Dispute," *Journal of International Trade and Commerce* (July 2009), https://www.usitc.gov/publications/332/journals/online_gambling_dispute.pdf

[2] Fareed Zakaria, "Culture Is Destiny: A Conversation with Lee Kuan Yew," *Foreign Affairs* 73, no. 2 (March/April 1994): 109.

CHAPTER 2
Small States and Economic Development

International organizations accord great relevance to the economic dimension of small states. Two landmark publications by the Commonwealth Secretariat, in particular, have framed evolving thinking on this broad issue. The first was published in 1985 under the title of *Vulnerability: Small States in the Global Society*. An updated version of this report, *A Future for Small States: Overcoming Vulnerability*, was published in 1997. This follow-on report focused more on economic and environmental vulnerabilities than its predecessor, which had focused primarily on traditional geopolitical and security vulnerabilities.[1]

By reframing the focus of its analysis on the international economic interests and vulnerabilities of small states over their international political (security) concerns, the updated 1997 Commonwealth report set the study of small states on a new path. Interestingly, this publication's new emphasis was reflected in organizational changes inside the Commonwealth Secretariat as responsibility for small states within the organization shifted from the Political Affairs Division to the Economics Affairs Division. Linked to these developments, a subsequent report of 2000 by the Commonwealth Secretariat-World Bank Joint Task Force on Small States noted that small states are more economically vulnerable than larger states due to their "special development challenges."[2]

---

1   Commonwealth Advisory Group, *A Future for Small States: Overcoming Vulnerability* (London: Commonwealth Secretariat, 1997), 177.
2   Commonwealth Secretariat/World Bank Joint Task Force, *Small States: Meeting Challenges in the Global Economy* (Washington, DC: World Bank, 2000). http://documents.worldbank.org/curated/en/267231468763824990/Small-states-meeting-challenges-in-the-global-economy.

In dealing with the economic context of small states, this chapter will examine how they develop economically in the face of structural and environmental vulnerabilities, and how their economic development provides them with security and influence as well as the stability and prosperity required to thrive. Though there are obvious exceptions, notably Israel and Switzerland, one can argue that in virtually all states that are small in territory and population, but are also generally considered not weak, it is economic rather than military power that has enabled these countries to overcome their inherent vulnerabilities. In the economic sphere, small states may be deemed relatively powerful (or potentially so) if they are industrially advanced (for example, Switzerland or Sweden) or possess energy resources (the oil and gas producers of Norway and the Arab Gulf) or have thrived on extensive trade (Singapore) or have established themselves as leaders in valued areas of expertise and technology (Luxembourg in financial services, Cuba in medicine, and Ireland and Israel in the high-technology sector).[1]

The role of economic resources in the exercise of national power and sovereignty is one of the central themes of the realist paradigm in international relations. However, resources of power, as addressed in the next chapter, go beyond the realm of tangible resources. Small states must innovate to meet the challenges they face due to the unequal distribution of power in the international system. They need to be more innovative, more diligent in their policy development and in the implementation of policies in a globalized world. Tonurist argues that despite globalization providing an open market and the possibility for small states to grow their economies, such openness can also be a disadvantage because it results in exposure to exogenous external shocks that sometimes lead to volatility.[2]

Briguglio et al. have examined the dichotomous economic vulnerability/resilience framework of small states in a globalized world.[3] In a subsequent

---

1   Jacqueline Braveboy-Wagner, "Opportunities and Limitations of the Exercise of Foreign Policy Power by a Very Small State: The Case of Trinidad and Tobago," *Cambridge Review of International Affairs* 23, no. 3 (2010): 407–427.
2   Piret Tonurist, "What Is a 'Small State' in a Globalising Economy?," *Halduskultuur – Administrative Culture* 11, no. 1 (2010): 8–29.
3   Lino Briguglio, Gordon Cordina, Nadia Farrugia and Stephanie Vella, "Economic Vulnerability and Resilience: Concepts and Measurements," *Oxford Development Studies* 37, no. 3 (2009): 229–247.

study, *A Vulnerability and Resilience Framework for Small States*, Briguglio introduced the concept of economic security within small states.[1] He argued that small states exemplify three dominant commonalities. The first is a "very high degree of economic openness due to dependence on exports and imports." This is a consequence of the fact that small states often have small domestic markets and may also lack indigenous natural resources. The second characteristic is a "high degree of export concentration, primarily due to their small economic size." This leads to constraints on the diversification of economic activities.[2] That said, countries like Norway and some member states of the Gulf Cooperation Council (GCC) have used their abundant energy resources to diversify their economies through the accumulation of sovereign wealth investment across the world.[3] The third, and last, of Briguglio's arguments is that small states demonstrate a "high dependence on strategic imports such as fuel and food."

All of the above can be perceived as vulnerabilities as they point to small states having a high exposure to external economic shocks. Other vulnerabilities include limitations in the ability to exploit economies of scale, develop effective competition on the domestic level, high transaction costs, including transport costs, insulation, and remoteness (especially for small island nations) and a significant susceptibility to natural disasters and climate change.[4]

Despite these challenges, Katzenstein in his seminal work argues that small states have the flexibility[5] to respond to vulnerabilities by building a consensus with domestic and international stakeholders. This view is restated in Denny Lewis-Bynoe's work which argues that a framework

---

1   Lino Briguglio, *A Vulnerability and Resilience Framework for Small States* (London: Commonwealth Secretariat, 2014).
2   Ibid.
3   Juergen Braunstein, "The Domestic Drivers of State Finance Institutions: Evidence from Sovereign Wealth Funds," *Review of International Political Economy* 26, no. 6 (2017): 980–1003.
4   Briguglio, *A Vulnerability and Resilience Framework for Small States*.
5   Peter J. Katzenstein, *Small States in World Markets: Industrial Policies in Europe* (Ithaca: Cornell University Press, 1985).

can be developed for small states to develop their resilience to economic shocks given their inherent, mostly size-based, vulnerabilities.[1]

Small state economies are therefore impacted by a range of dichotomous forces that they must manage in ways that larger actors, especially highly developed ones with strong economic governance, can avoid. This is why Haskin indicates that the inherent vulnerabilities of small states (again small island states in particular) will always affect their economic development, though like Katzenstein and Lewis-Bynoe, he does acknowledge that they can build resilience through cooperation and economic policies that exploit their strengths.[2]

Conceptualization of Small State Economic Resources

Balaam and Veseth define international political economy as "the tension between the market, where individuals engage in self-interested activities, and the state, where those same individuals undertake collective action …."[3] This illuminates that there are two dominant drivers of international political economy: self-interested individuals and the political institutions of the state. The fact that the above definition refers to an underlying tension, serves as a reminder that there exists a conflictual relationship between the market and the state.

However, this definition precludes other geopolitical factors[4] and the extent that the state's actions can either exacerbate existing economic vulnerabilities or facilitate economic resilience. For this reason, Balaam and Dillman argue that "international political economy involves tensions amongst a variety of states, market and societal actors and institutions."[5]

---

1   Denny Lewis-Bynoe (ed.) *Building the Resilience of Small States: A Revised Framework* (London: Commonwealth Secretariat, 2014).
2   Jeffery Haskins, "Building in Small Island Economies: From Vulnerabilities to Opportunities," *CTA Policy Brief* 8 (2012):1–4.
3   David N. Balaam and Michael Veseth, *Introduction to International Political Economy* (Upper Saddle River, NJ: Prentice Hall, 1996).
4   Timothy C. Lim, *International Political Economy: An Introduction to Approaches, Regimes and Issues* (Washington DC: Saylor Foundation, 2014).
5   David N. Balaam and Bradford Dillman, *Introduction to International Political Economy* (Boston: Longman, 2011).

They extend the definition of actors in the international political economy to include the state, societal and non-state actors. They also mention explicitly "corporations, labor unions, social movements, criminal organizations, nongovernmental organizations (NGOs), religious institutions and epistemic communities."[1]

For small states, their own vulnerabilities and the existence of such a broad range of actors that they need to engage with, and navigate around, can create significant challenges, especially for developing and less developed actors. As Lee and Smith argue: By presenting small states as a problem to be solved, vulnerability discourses divert attention away from the existence of unequal power structures that far from being the natural result of smallness, are in fact contingent and politically contested.[2] Despite the inherent vulnerability of small states, they have opportunities through their own political systems and international organizations to utilize their opportunities as well as to develop the resilience required to deal with exogenous shocks.

As was noted in other contexts in the previous chapter, there exists a misconception that stems from debates on the inherent smallness of states in relation to material reality and how this reality limits their capabilities to influence geopolitical and economic issues. This is particularly true because a small state's capacity and influence cannot be measured, again as noted in the previous chapter, only in terms of fixed quantitative attributes such as GDP, population or geographic size. For this reason, Magnusdottir and Thorhallsson indicate that in "comparing the perceptual size of the Nordic EU members, one should not focus on the differences in their fixed size (i.e., their population size) but rather on what factors have formed their self-perception and other actors' perceptions of them."[3] These perceptions can create a dependency complex; for example, Ilyin has argued that small states tend to adjust their international relationships

---

1 Lim, *International Political Economy*, 13.
2 Lee and Smith, "Small State Discourses in the International Political Economy," 1091.
3 Gunnhirdur L. Magnusdottir and Baldur Thorhallsson, "The Nordic States and Agenda-Setting in the European Union: How Do Small States Score?," *Stjornmal & Stjornsysla* 1, no. 7 (2011): 204–226.

to fit their relative "size."[1] Smirnov, on the other hand, argues that interdependence has not only made it possible for small states to adjust their geopolitical positions but has also impacted on the decisions of more powerful and larger actors in the system.[2]

Whether one chooses to use quantitative, qualitative or relational criteria to characterize small states, it is undeniable that all small states, however conceived and measured, must negotiate concepts such as power, influence and self-image to enable them to deal successfully with their external environments.[3] This does not, however, discount the hierarchical international environment that constrains small states economically, as well as politically, in different ways. This can depend on the structural hierarchy imposed by the dominant material reality that is often expressed in statistical tables published by powerful states and international organizations such as the UN, the WTO or the Commonwealth.

Such realities underscore the unequal power structure in the international system and the inherent weaknesses of small states regardless of the choice of definitions. It also runs the risk of transforming the debate over small state economic resources into a dichotomous vulnerability/resilience discourse. Even outliers among small states, such as Qatar and the Nordic nations, that have used either their energy resources or innovative capacity to change their economic and geopolitical standing, remain prone not only to the domestic and external challenges mentioned above, but also to perceptions of weakness. In acknowledgement of this, the remainder of this chapter focuses on small states' economic resources and the role that vulnerability and resilience play, especially when external shocks occur.

---

1   M. V. Ilyin, "Is a Universal Typology of States Possible?," *Political Science* 4, no. 8 (2008): 41.
2   Vadim Smirnov, "The Role of Small Countries in Post-Soviet Territorial Restructuring: The Baltic Case," *Baltic Region* 4, no. 22 (2014): 42–49.
3   Michael W. Mosser, "Engineering Influence: The Subtle Power of Small States in the CSCE/OSCE," in *Small States and Alliances*, ed. E. Reiter and H. Gartner (Leiden: Springer, 2001), 63–84.

The Economic Vulnerabilities of Small States

The extent that small states are disadvantaged due to their economic vulnerabilities is a contested concept in the literature. The argument of Briguglio and others that smallness denotes susceptibility to being "harmed by external economic forces as a result of exposure to such forces"[1] has been widely accepted. However, the heterogeneous nature of small states means that it is not sufficient to adopt IR approaches that typically tend to emphasize the realist ontological view of small states as nothing more than static and vulnerable economic actors. Bishop, in seeking to delineate the political economy of small states with regards to their vulnerabilities, argues the need to rethink their "capabilities," "institutions" and "relations" by considering the variety of theoretical approaches in IR.[2]

These theoretical approaches, as the next chapter will show, include liberalism, intuitionalism, and constructivism, as well as realism. Ingebritsen argues that by considering the spectrum of IR theories that can be applied to small states, it provides an opportunity to consider these states as economic "norm entrepreneurs" acting in different ways than larger actors.[3] Various scholarly research on small states, including the work of Briguglio and others referenced above, provide varying conceptualizations of small state vulnerabilities that stem from their inherent smallness, insularity and geographic remoteness.[4]

These vulnerabilities can include, but are not limited to, "natural disasters; currency crises; dramatic environmental degradation; high transaction costs; price fluctuations in commodity markets, especially oil;

---

1 Briguglio, *A Vulnerability and Resilience Framework for Small States*, 7.
2 Matthew L. Bishop, "The Political Economy of Small States: Enduring Vulnerability?," *Review of International Political Economy* 19, no. 5 (2012): 942–960.
3 Christine Ingebritsen, "Conclusion: Learning from Lilliput," in *Small States in International Relations*, eds. Christine Ingebritsen, Iver B. Neumann, Sieglinde Gstohl and Jessica Beyer (Seattle, WA: University of Washington Press, 2006), 289–292.
4 Lino Briguglio, "Small Island States and Their Economic Vulnerabilities," *World Development* 23 (1995): 1615–1632.

weak administration; high levels of migration, and volatile GDP growth."[1] This supports the conclusions of the International Monetary Fund (IMF) report, *Macroeconomic Issues in Small States and Implications for Fund Engagement*. This illuminating study argues that the intrinsic characteristics of small state economies include challenges such as high fixed costs in the public sector in relation to diseconomies of scale; high fixed costs in the private sector as a result of the limited size of small states' economies; and less favorable access to the global capital market as a result of their fixed costs and susceptibility to volatility.

An additional factor identified by the above IMF study is susceptibility to natural disasters, with many small states being prone to earthquakes and hurricanes as a result of their locations.[2] In particular, it has been shown that the human cost of such disasters on small states disproportionately affect their economies and their ability to influence the international system, effectively making them rule-and price-takers. As Briguglio sums up, "The negative effects of downside shocks in the real world leads to declines in the real GDP of poor countries from which it is difficult to recover."[3] In particular, they can increase unemployment and poverty, which result in malnutrition, health problems and possibly higher mortality rates.

The argument that the extensive vulnerabilities of small states are detrimental to their economies is linked to the view that these vulnerabilities are inherent characteristics of an economy and, as such, can be either permanent or quasi-permanent.[4] One implication of this is that while small states may well have economic vulnerabilities, they do not necessarily entail a low level of GDP per capita or high levels of instability. This is due to the fact that those vulnerabilities that do exist

---

1 Bishop, "The Political Economy of Small States: Enduring Vulnerability?," 948.
2 International Monetary Fund, *Macroeconomic Issues in Small States and Implications for Fund Engagement* (Washington DC, IMF, 2013).
3 Lino Briguglio, *Growth with Resilience: Perspective from the Commonwealth and Francophonie and Recommendation to the G20* (London: Commonwealth Secretariat, 2011).
4 Briguglio, "Small Island States and Their Economic Vulnerabilities," 1620.

are only some of the important economic variables.[1] Therefore, a small state economy could be highly vulnerable, but it could also register relatively high income per capita and relatively low income-volatility. Briguglio refers to this as the "Singapore Paradox," a situation in which a seemingly vulnerable small country leverages its location and policy competency to achieve economic success.[2]

The case of Singapore, and of other seemingly successful small states, has underscored the extent that the discourse on negative consequences of small state vulnerabilities can be challenged. Cordina, for example, disagrees with authors such as Baldacchino about small state economic vulnerability on the basis of possible misspecification rather than actual economic realities. Instead, Cordina argues that even a vulnerable small state can have a viable and successful economy if, like Singapore, it develops the appropriate policy mechanisms.[3]

The tension in the literature relating to small state vulnerabilities is visible when one considers Bishop's point that small states have the ability to engage in a variety of productive activities that are profitable and that would, as such, support their economic growth.[4] This does not invalidate, as Payne argues, the fact that even economically successful small states cannot fundamentally change their intrinsic vulnerabilities.[5] The existence of intrinsic vulnerability alongside economic success as well as relatively high levels of development can be seen in the cases of Iceland, Antigua-Barbuda, St. Lucia and the Maldives. All provide empirical evidence of

---

1   Lino Briguglio, "Economic Vulnerability and Resilience: Concepts and Measurements," in *Vulnerability and Resilience of Small States*, eds. L. Briguglio and E. J. Kisanga (London: Commonwealth Secretariat and the University of Malta, 2004), 43–53.
2   Ibid.
3   Gordon Cordina, "The Macroeconomic and Growth Dynamics of Small States," in *Small States: Economic Review & Basic Statistics* (London: Commonwealth Secretariat, 2008), 21–37.
4   Bishop, "The Political Economy of Small States: Enduring Vulnerability?," 952.
5   Antony Payne, "Afterword: Vulnerability as a Condition, Resilience as a Strategy," in *The Diplomacies of Small States: Between Vulnerability and Resilience*, eds. A. F. Cooper and T. M. Shaw (Basingstoke: Palgrave MacMillan, 2009).

the fact that vulnerability and resilience can co-exist.[1] Policy choices and good governance may support small state economies, but this requires innovation not only in economic development but diplomacy and shared fortune in avoiding often unavoidable natural disasters.

Others have argued that vulnerability can even provide an economic advantage for small states. Armstrong and Read have demonstrated that on average small states enjoy higher levels of per capita GDP than larger states and that, on this basis at least, size does not systematically become a barrier to economic development. To further support their argument, the same authors also note that Briguglio's 1995 vulnerability index correlates positively with GDP per capita.[2]

This argument can be juxtaposed with that made by Baldacchino and Bertram, who have argued that the small state vulnerability argument is diplomatically driven and is deterministic in associating small states with weakness. They further assert that the "strategic flexibility" of small states provides them with endogenous incentives to adapt and strengthen their economies.[3] Easterly and Kraay's work on the advantages of small state economies points to the fact that small states can position themselves to diversify away from the risk of shocks.[4] Lee and Smith argue, as indicated earlier in this chapter, that the "inherent vulnerability" discourses of small states divert attention from the real issue of the unequal global power structures.[5]

In his study of how small states use international organizations to manage the consequences of exogenous shocks, André Broome argues that

---

1   Bishop, "The Political Economy of Small States: Enduring Vulnerability?," 953.
2   Harvey W. Armstrong and Robert Read, "The Phantom of Liberty? Economic Growth and the Vulnerability of Small States," *Journal of International Development* 14, no. 4 (2002): 435–458.
3   Godfrey Baldacchino and Geoff Bertram, "The Beak of the Finch: Insights into the Economic Development of Small Economies," *Round Table: The Commonwealth Journal of International Affairs* 98, no. 401 (2009): 141–160.
4   William Easterly and Aart C. Kraay, "Small States, Small Problems? Income, Growth and Volatility in Small States," *World Development* 28, no. 11 (2002): 2013–2027.
5   Lee and Smith, "Small State Discourses in the International Political Economy," 1091.

the case of Iceland's negotiations with the IMF for crisis management support during the 2008 financial crisis demonstrates that while small states can potentially build economies of scale in specialist sectors such as banking, the risks inherent in rapid financial expansion greatly increase their vulnerability to external shocks. In such circumstances, small states are likely to struggle to level the playing field in their attempts to negotiate the constraints and opportunities provided by engagement with the IMF in periods of international crisis, during which they face higher stakes compared with larger economies and have a narrower set of policy choices at their disposal.[1]

Small States Economics—Resilience

Briguglio has argued that one key question to ask is whether "resilience-building is automatically triggered in small economies or is a matter of choice."[2] He expounds on this point by distinguishing between causes and effects, and makes the case that it is possible to develop policies of resilience-building that mitigate such manifestations. However, the real question relates to "resistance" and "economic resistance" in particular and how it applies to small state economics? Resilience has been defined in various ways, making the concept somewhat unclear when applied to economic matters. This is particularly the case because without specific parameters to measure, the concept can become subjective.

However, given that some of a small state's national resources such as self-perception and self-image are subjective, as the next chapter will address, it is safe to assume that economic resilience is not always measurable. This is because resilience is a relative concept even in its accepted definition. The *Oxford Advanced Learner's Dictionary*, for example, defines it both as "the ability of a people or things to feel better quickly after something unpleasant" and "the ability of a substance to return to its original shape after it has been bent."

---

[1] André Broome, "Negotiating Crisis: The IMF and Disaster Capitalism in Small States," *The Round Table: The Commonwealth Journal of International Affairs* 100, no. 413 (2011): 155–167.

[2] Briguglio, *A Vulnerability and Resilience Framework for Small States*, 10.

In seeking to conceptualize economic resilience, Briguglio et al. argue that there are three frameworks that can be applied. These include the "ability of an economy to recover quickly," the "ability to withstand shocks" and the "ability of an economy to avoid shocks." The first one involves flexibility which enables an economy to bounce back after being affected by a shock. This has been termed the "shock-counteraction" characteristic of an economy.[1] It requires a pre-existing strong fiscal position or the adoption of appropriate policies such as tax cuts to counter the negative impact of shocks. Hallegatte refers to such economic flexibility as "dynamic resilience."[2] The second context suggests the absorption or the neutralization of the adverse effect of shocks to an economy. This could involve the ability to quickly shift resources to an economic sector with strong demand. The third context involves the inherent nature of an economy and therefore the opposite of vulnerability.[3]

Economic resilience in small states requires, somewhat contradictorily, the development of flexibility and rigidity that provide an environment capable of adapting and rebounding. This is in accordance with the hypothesis of Briguglio et al. that economic resilience building policies involve the capture of five variables: macroeconomic stability, market efficiency, good political governance, social development and environmental governance.[4] This aligns with the argument of Greenham et al. that resilient economies have the following characteristics: social qualities, including the capacity to develop social and human capital; interdependence and localization that can bring about a balance between local and interconnected variables; diversity across national social,

---

1   Lino Briguglio, Gordon Cordina, Stephanie Bugeja and Nadia Farrugia, *Conceptualising and Measuring Economic Resilience* (Valetta: University of Malta, 2006).
2   Stephane Hallegatte, "Economic Resilience—Definition and Measurement," Policy Research Working Paper 6852 (Washington DC: The World Bank, 2014).
3   Briguglio et al., *Conceptualising and Measuring Economic Resilience*.
4   Briguglio, Cordina, Farrugia and Stephanie Vella, "Economic Vulnerability and Resilience: Concepts and Measurements," 229.

economic and financial systems; and innovation, centered around learning and adaptation.[1]

Small states that develop such capabilities can, as Singapore has done, play a significant role in the international economic system. The importance of macroeconomic stability to economic resilience in a small state can be seen in its relationship to fiscal deficits and debt, a healthy balance of payments and GDP volatility. It is far more likely for small states with economic resilience strategies to achieve a healthy fiscal position with regards to government budgets. Additionally, low unemployment and inflation as well as the external debt-GDP ratio are a function of policies that in turn underpin a nation's resilience.[2] In the small state context, for example, Brito has demonstrated how control over these issues is an important determinant of economic growth and a driver of resilience.[3]

Hnatkovska and Loayza's macroeconomic stability study reveals a negative relationship between economic stability and growth, especially for poor countries with challenging institutional situations and weak financial development.[4] Sirimaneetham and Temple also show similar results in their study of seventy developing countries which indicated that economic growth is associated with macroeconomic stability.[5] Other studies, including those of Armstrong and Read, and Yang et al.,[6] have

---

1. Tony Greenham, Elizabeth Cox and Josh Ryan-Collins, *Mapping Economic Resilience* (York: Friends Provident Foundation, 2013).
2. Briguglio, *A Vulnerability and Resilience Framework for Small States*.
3. Joao Brito, "Country Size and Determinants of Economic Growth: A Survey with Special Interest on Small States," MPRA Paper, No. 61273, 2015.
4. Viktoria V. Hnatkovska and Norman Loayza, "Volatility and Growth," World Bank Policy Research Working Paper No. 3184 (Washington DC: World Bank, 2004).
5. Vatcharin Sirimaneetham and Jonathan R. W. Temple, "Macroeconomic Stability and the Distribution of Growth Rates," *World Bank Economic Review* 23, no. 3 (2009): 443–479.
6. Harvey W. Armstrong and Robert Read, "The Determinants of Economic Growth in Small States," *The Round Table: The Commonwealth Journal of International Affairs* 92, no. 368 (2003): 99–124; Yongzheng Yang, Hong Chen, Shiuraj Singh and Baljeet Singh, "The Pacific Speed of Growth: How Fast Can It Be and What Determines It?," IMF working Paper 13, no. 104 (2013).

shown that small states' economic growth is positively correlated with macroeconomic stability. Therefore, the proper development of a resilient small state economy requires macroeconomic stability. In other words, a stable economy provides scope for growth and those policies and practices that contribute to this should be factored into the economic governance of small states to provide for resilience.

Another determinant of economic resilience in small states is market efficiency, which refers to the flexibility that allows supply and demand to adjust as rapidly as possible so that market forces can find an equilibrium. Cordina's occasional paper on *Economic Resilience and Market Efficiency in Small States* is focused on small island states. Nonetheless, it provides an excellent overview of why market efficiency is a strong indicator of a small state's economic resilience. The market provides the means for the allocation of resources—labor, capital, goods or services. Cordina mentions Malta, Cyprus and Singapore as good examples of market-driven resilient economies.[1] Such efficiency requires a properly functioning market that can claim the full participation of the private sector and robust competition. The challenge here for small states relates to market size, although globalization has made it easier for innovative small states that are willing and able to adapt to overcome this obstacle to some extent.

An independent legal system must also be in place so that investors in the economy and other stakeholders are confident that their rights will be protected at all times.[2] Alongside a good legal framework, an economically resilient small state requires good political governance. This includes a capacity to safeguard the political, economic and institutional processes of the state in ways that ensure that the rights of citizens and other stakeholders are upheld.[3] Good political governance is associated with efficiency, transparency, accountability and participation which provides

---

1 Gordon Cordina, "Economic Resilience and Market Efficiency in Small States," in *Small States and the Pillars of Economic Resilience*, eds. L. Briguglio, G. Cordina, N. Farrugia and C. Vigilance (Valletta: Islands and Small States Institute, University of Malta, 2008).

2 Norman V. Loayza and Raimundo Soto, *On the Measurement of Market-Oriented Reforms* (Washington DC: World Bank, 2003).

3 Ibid.

a roadmap for stability. Using the Kaufmann Index for Good Governance, which considers among other things, regulatory quality, control of corruption and the rule of law, Curmi has been able to demonstrate the important role that good governance plays in contributing to the economic resilience of small states. Those small actors that scored well on the Kaufmann Index in Curmi's study include Iceland, Luxemburg, Andorra, Malta and Barbados, while those with the worst scores were Equatorial Guinea, Comoros, Timor Leste, Djibouti and Gabon.[1]

In addition to the economic resilience parameters discussed above, Briguglio also emphasizes the importance of social development. This includes education and health measured as "the non-income components of the Human Development Index."[2] Social development and social cohesion are also considered essential elements of economic resilience and Vandemoortele argues that there is a "positive relationship between social harmony and macroeconomic stability."[3]

Andreasson has also shown the importance of social harmony and trust for the economic resilience of small states by distinguishing its positive contribution to those countries where it is prevalent, notably the Nordic countries of Denmark, Finland, Iceland, Norway and Sweden, from other countries around the world, even those in Western Europe with similar levels of social welfare but much lower levels of social trust.[4] On a related point, Andreasson and others, like Foa, have argued that high levels of social trust make possible a reduction in transaction costs in the market because it eliminates the need for verification and other added costs.[5] Additionally, social development and cohesion have been shown to

---

1   Liliana Curmi, "Governance and Small States," in *Occasional Papers on Islands and Small States* (Valletta: Island and Small States Institute, University of Malta, 2009).

2   Briguglio, *A Vulnerability and Resilience Framework for Small States*, 22.

3   Milo Vandemoortele, *Equity: A Key to Macroeconomic Stability* (London: Overseas Development Institute, 2010).

4   Ulf Andreasson, *Trust—the Nordic Gold* (Copenhagen: Nordic Council of Ministers, 2017).

5   Roberto Foa, *The Economic Rationale for Social Cohesion—The Cross-Country Evidence*, International Conference on Social Cohesion (OECD, Paris, 2011).

promote collective action that supports infrastructure development, education and health.¹

Baldacchino argues that social capital or cohesion—the resourcefulness of a nation's citizens to respond positively, collectively and responsibly to socio-economic challenges—explains positive socio-economic development in small states.² Europe is full of small states with high levels of social capital. Every year since 1990, the United Nations Development Program (UNDP) has published the Human Development Index (HDI). This evaluates a country's economic and social progress outside of traditional GDP measures. Instead, the HDI considers education, in particular the literacy levels of the local population, alongside health indicators, notably access to clean water and electricity, and basic health and sanitation facilities as well as life expectancy at birth.

Though the HDI does not consider gender or income inequality or human and political rights, it is nonetheless accepted as an important and valuable measure of socio-economic development above and beyond GDP. The UNDP classifies countries into three groups: (1) high human development (with a HDI measure between 0.8 and 1.0, largely for industrialized countries); (2) medium human development (a HDI between 0.5 and 0.8); and (3) low human development (a HDI less than 0.5).

In the period between 1995 and 2019, no single country achieved the full mark of 1.0, though a number of small European states scored very highly each year. Notably Norway, Iceland, Switzerland and Ireland consistently ranked in the top five globally over this period with Norway topping the rankings on several occasions. Other small states that regularly appear in the top-ten include Hong Kong and Singapore. What all these states have in common is a set of policy choices that have looked to introduce and sustain national development strategies that deal with and attempt to overcome exactly the same small state challenges that rapidly developing states continue to face—a limited domestic market, high

---

1 Ibid.
2 Godfrey Baldacchino, "The Contribution of "Social Capital" to Economic Growth: Lessons from Island Jurisdictions," *The Round Table: The Commonwealth Journal of International Affairs* 94, 378 (2005): 31–46.

production costs, low economies of scale, a lack of exportable products, and low levels of industrial production.[1]

Another salient element of economic resilience for small states is environmental management which has been defined as "institutions, regulation, practices and other processes conducive to environmental conservation, protection and the use of natural resources."[2] The link between environmental management and economic resilience for small states is based on the ability of an economy to recover from major external shocks. It can have a positive impact on the market, social development and social cohesion, all of which can nurture economic resilience in a small state.

As noted in the first chapter, environmental management is a particularly salient consideration for small island states given their need to adapt to climate change threats which could have potentially devastating effects on their survival.[3] Even if climate change does not have an existential impact on these states, studies published by the IMF indicate that small developing countries are usually disproportionately affected by natural disasters and that, on average, such disasters bring about a 2 percent reduction in GDP. It has also been shown that approximately 9 percent of all disasters in small states cause damage and destruction that equates to 30 percent of GDP.[4]

This data indicates that economic resilience in a small state is not sustainable if environmental protection is not addressed as a national priority that is integral to economic and social development. Acevedo's empirical study of small island states in the Caribbean has shown how higher levels of public debt have been a direct consequence of flooding.[5]

---

1 Michael Handel, *Weak States in the International System* (London: Frank Cass, 1981), 220–229.
2 Briguglio, *A Vulnerability and Resilience Framework for Small States*, 24.
3 IPCC, "Small Islands," *IPCC Fourth Assessment Report—Working Group II: Impacts, Adaptation and Vulnerability*, Geneva, Switzerland, Intergovernmental Panel on Climate Change, 2007.
4 *Small States' Resilience to Natural Disasters and Climate Change—Role for the IMF* (Washington DC, International Monetary Fund, 2016).
5 Sebastian Acevedo, "Debt, Growth, and Natural Disasters: A Caribbean Trilogy," IMF Working Paper No. 14/125 (Washington DC, International Monetary Fund, 2014).

Similar studies by Lee et al. have also shown how natural disasters have resulted in increased public indebtedness across the small island states of the Pacific.[1] However, the challenge for small states is not simply a lack of resources to fight climate change. Environmental management cannot be a local issue only, and collective action is required by small states to ensure that other international actors come to view environmental management as a global priority.

Economic Resources and the Geopolitical Disposition of Small States

The vital role of economic resources in contributing to a state's influence and power in the international system stems from its convertibility into different elements of power.[2] Smallness, however defined, can determine the feasibility of a state's capacity to exercise compulsory, institutional, structural and productive power. Mosser illustrated this in a study of the Organization for Security and Cooperation in Europe (OSCE), where the formal rules of the organization provide for consensus decision-making. However, the hierarchical geopolitical system is still largely influenced by the great powers. This means that small states and micro states such as Liechtenstein and San Marino must engineer their influence to the best of their abilities in order to influence the decision-making process of organizations that they participate in.

Mohammadzadeh has also examined influence engineering and economic resilience in the case of Qatar, a small state with the highest per capita income in the world, whose resources have enabled it to carve out a niche position of relative influence in international affairs.[3] Qatar, for

---

1 Dongyeol Lee, Patrizia Tumbarello, Kazuaki Washimi and Tlek Zeinullayev, "Mind the Gap: Public Investment, Growth and Natural Disaster Risk in the Small States of the Pacific," Working Paper (Washington DC, International Monetary Fund, 2016).
2 Michael Barnett and Raymond Duvall, "Power in International Politics," *International Organisation* 59, no. 1 (2005): 39–75.
3 Babak Mohammadzadeh, "Status and Foreign Policy Change in Small States: Qatar's Emergence in Perspective," *The International Spectator: Italian Journal of International Affairs* 52, no. 2 (2017): 19–36.

example, cooperates with Iran while simultaneously providing military bases for American and Turkish troops. Cooper and Shaw have shown that although a small state's vulnerability narrative may affect their self-image, they can be strong economic actors in international relations if they behave innovatively. They can take advantage of the formal rules of the international system to win non-military conflicts, even those they engage in with larger regional actors and great powers.[1]

While these arguments emphasize how small state economies can be both vulnerable and resilient at the same time, the international political economy discourse of small states is replete with the inherent vulnerability narrative that reinforces the perception of smallness. However, the unequal nature of power relations in the international system forces ambitious small states to be innovative in their quest for influence in a globalized world. This is especially true given that, as Lee and Smith argue, "Discourses yield material effects."[2]

These material effects are born out of the unique challenges that small states face. In the process, these challenges also provide an opportunity for rapid learning that can be applied to economic development across a wide range of sectors. In other words, while the issue of inherent vulnerability exists in small state discourse, the role of small states in the international system is one that can be enhanced by policy choices that promote economic resilience and in turn can support a nation's ability to influence international affairs.

In support of this hypothesis, Auty highlights the different paths taken by Mauritius, and Trinidad and Tobago since the 1960s. Mauritius faced a challenging future in the early 1960s, but by subsequently adopting a competitive industrialization policy, it became increasingly resilient in economic terms.[3] Trinidad and Tobago, on the other hand, did not

---

1 Cooper and Shaw, "The Diplomacies of Small States at the Start of the Twenty-first Century," 28.
2 Lee and Smith, "Small State Discourses in the International Political Economy," 1101.
3 Richard M. Auty, "Natural Resources and Small Island Economies: Mauritius and Trinidad and Tobago," *Journal of Development Studies* 53, no. 2 (2017): 264–277.

implement policies that optimized its economic opportunities and valuable natural resources. This resulted in rent dependency and a struggle to address the staple trap, which is a reliance on the export of staples.[1]

This chapter has provided a conceptual overview of challenges and opportunities that small states face in developing their economies and attaining the necessary levels of resilience to protect their economic achievements. Despite their uniqueness in the international political economy, especially in light of the unequal distribution of geopolitical power, small states have the capacity in a globalized world to grow their economies through market expansion. Globalization provides such an opportunity with notable caveats including transaction costs, market protection and other weaknesses.

That said, this chapter has also challenged the traditionally prevalent discourse on the inherent vulnerability of small states by showing that there are many opportunities for them to move beyond the limitations of smallness and a self-image of demur incapacity. The "Singapore Paradox" provides a reminder that smallness does not necessarily have to equate to vulnerability or poor or limited economic development. Rather, small states can thrive economically in ways that afford them far greater influence in the international system than many larger states. As Briguglio has put it, even vulnerabilities provide a small state with advantages as well as disadvantages[2] and these can be exploited to increase economic capacity, reputation and influence.

This is not to deny the unequal hierarchical power structure of the global system or the resilience of this power imbalance. It does, however, point to the fact that small state policies that result in good macroeconomic management, good governance, social development, efficient markets and environmental management can serve to bolster economic resilience despite the unequal power dynamic. This is an important contributing factor to influence in the international system especially if it facilitates small states in becoming more resilient to external shocks. Economic power is, in the final account, an important form of power in the real

---

1 Ibid.
2 Briguglio, *A Vulnerability and Resilience Framework for Small States*, 7–8.

world, as Barnett and Duvall have shown in their research on the taxonomies of power.[1] As such, the more that a small state is able to negotiate the vulnerability-resilience axis, the greater potential it has to gain influence on a variety of geopolitical issues.

As Braveboy-Wagner has summed up, there remains, even into the contemporary era, a widely-held conventional view that the "universe of small states with the potential to exercise military or economic power is itself very small."[2] While small states may not be able to change the rules of the international system, there are different ways to think about small state power. Small states are by no means completely powerless in today's complex environment and may exert global as well as regional influence under the right circumstances. As this book argues throughout, there are a variety of small countries, including but by no means limited to Qatar, Singapore and the Nordic countries, that use their economic power to influence the international system in ways that have often been considered unavailable to small states.

---

1 Barnett and Duvall, "Power in International Politics," 39–75.
2 Braveboy-Wagner, "Opportunities and Limitations of the Exercise of Foreign Policy Power by a Very Small State: The Case of Trinidad and Tobago," 408.

CHAPTER 3
Small States and National Resources

The debate over definitions of small states, as illuminated in chapter 1, demonstrates the diversity that exists in how we understand the meaning of small in the international system. This diversity also extends to the issue of national resources in small states. In seeking to provide an overview of the institutional theory of resources in classical economics, Gregori notes that resources, including land and mineral deposits, are "natural" and given. This means that in the global sense they are material, fixed and finite.[1] However, from the institutionalist perspective "resources are not, they become" as indicated in the thinking of Clarence Ayres and Erich Zimmermann. As the process of resource-becoming is both ideational and material, it follows that such resources cannot be assumed to be fixed or finite.[2]

This underscores the fact that national resources in the small state can be abstract and intangible as well as concrete or material. It is on this basis that Gregori argues that resources require the creative process that fashions material and non-material aspects into a form that is useful and serviceable to people. Resources are therefore "the sum total of human knowledge and capability."[3] This supports Mitchell's suggestion that the greatest resource is the human resource, and it is underpinned by knowledge and capacity.[4]

---

1. Thomas R. De Gregori, "Resources Are Not; They Become: An Institutional Theory," *Journal of Economic Issues* XXI, no. 3 (1987): 1241–1263.
2. Ibid.
3. Ibid.
4. Wesley C. Mitchell, "Conservation, Liberty and Economics," in *The Foundations of Conservation Education* (New York: National Wildlife Federation, 1941), 1.

For this reason, the power of a nation-state is still widely understood in terms of resources. Liina Areng argues that, "The size of a state has generally been seen as directly connected to its capabilities and influence in international politics."[1] This underplays the fact that small states have both tangible and intangible resources that provide, and increase, their capabilities to be active agents in international politics. This chapter examines the conceptual framework of small state national resources in the context of a number of international relations theories, our understanding of power and the role of national resources in small state foreign policies.

Conceptual Frameworks of National Resources

National resources as instruments of power are a complex mix of concrete and abstract phenomena. For small states in international politics, national resources in all their forms must be utilized intelligently to enable them to have the influence they seek. However, Hayter and Patchell argue that contemporary definitions of resources continue to take their cues from Zimmermann's dictum that "resources are not, they become."[2] Bridge agrees on the grounds that resources are not "givens" but rather a "culturally mediated appraisal of the physical environment" shaped by factors such as the economy, political institutions, social attributes and belief systems.[3]

This perspective overlaps with three of the core assumptions in realist theoretical paradigms of international relations as set down by Legro and Moravcsik: That the actor is a rational unitary political unit that exists in anarchy; that state preferences are fixed and there are uniformly conflictual goals; and that material capabilities have primacy in the system.[4]

---

1   Liina Areng, "Lilliputian States in Digital Affairs and Cyber Security," *The Tallinn Papers* 4 (2014): 1–12.
2   Roger Hayter and Jerry Patchell, "Resources Geography," in *International Encyclopaedia of the Social & Behavioural Sciences*, 2nd ed., ed. James D. Wright (Oxford: Elsevier, 2015), 568–575.
3   Gavin Bridge, "Resource Geography," in *International Encyclopaedia of Social and Behavioural Sciences*, ed. Wright, 1326–1329.
4   Jeffery W. Legro and Andrew Moravcsik, "Is Anybody Still a Realist?," *International Security* 24, no. 2 (1999): 5–55.

This core ontological position of realism in which material and objective reality take preference over other tools of power entails "that control over material resources in world politics lies at the core of realism" and the international relations of states.[1] Small states are, of course, heterogeneous. Some have an abundance of material resources and others a severe lack. This means that the international power balance favors the larger and more powerful states of the period, such as the United States, China, and Russia in the contemporary era. However, Morgenthau lists the elements of power which include "geography, natural resources, industrial capacity, military preparedness, population, national character and morale, the quality of diplomacy and government."[2] This, in turn, suggests that small states have a wide variety of resources that can help them to garner influence in the international political system.

This view is supported by Thorhallsson's multifunctional framework which categorizes small states into six silos.[3] The first is fixed size which refers to the territorial and population size of the state. The second is sovereignty, which refers to the ability of a small state to maintain control over its territory so that it can govern without outside interference. Political size is the third category, and refers to the military and administrative capabilities of the state, including its capacity to develop consensus around its foreign policy, and the ability to have and maintain the domestic cohesion required to tackle and solve problems. For example, as the two case study chapters below will demonstrate, when Qatar was blockaded by Saudi Arabia, Egypt, the UAE and Bahrain in June 2017, the country's resilience was achieved through the management of its natural gas reserves and its sovereign wealth fund alongside high levels of domestic stability. All three national resources ensured that Qatar held firm in the face of political and economic isolation and garnered both regional and international support to continue to provide for its people.

---

1   Ibid.
2   Peter Sutch and Juanita Elias, *International Relations: The Basics* (New York: Routledge, 2007), 49.
3   Baldur Thorhallsson, "The Size of States in the European Union: Theoretical and Conceptual Perspectives," *Journal of European Integration* 28, no.1 (2006): 7–31.

A further category is perceptual size. This goes beyond the size of the small state's GDP and the level of its development and includes the resource-value of political self-perception and discourse that citizens, groups, leaders and the public maintain in regard to their state. The more a small state perceives itself as having influence in international affairs, the more likely it is to have such a role.[1] Such perceptions, while being projected from within, must also be projected onto other states to maximize effectiveness. Thorhallsson's final category is preference size, which refers to "the specific ideas, ambitions and priorities that elites in the state have and how expansive they are."[2]

These categories underscore the fact that in discussing and critiquing the small state resources that support their abilities or capacities to influence the international system, the materialistic paradigm of the realist international relations theory is salient but limited. It does not fully explain how a number of diverse small states like Singapore, Norway, Switzerland, Ireland, Liberia, and some of the Gulf Cooperation Council (GCC) members as well as many others, individually and collectively exert influence in international politics.

Therefore, in seeking to conceptualize small state national resources, it is important that the issue is examined from a broader perspective that transcends the narrow realist materialistic paradigm. This not only involves examining Thorhallsson's schematic categorization framework of small states but also requires an overview of some of the other foundational international relations theories. Small state national resources could therefore be conceptualized from the premises of fixed size, sovereignty size, political size, economic size, perceptual size or preference size or a combination of all or some, alongside theoretical paradigms in IR such as realism, liberalism, institutionalism and constructivism. Additionally, scholars of small states have also proposed status-seeking theory and shelter theory to determine the actions of these states in the international political arena.[3]

---

1   Thorhallsson, "The Size of States in the European Union," 24.
2   Ibid.
3   Ibid.

The challenge for such paradigmatic development is trying to ensure that there is coherence and distinctiveness because, as Legro and Moravcsik argue, these qualities are salient if a paradigm is to be "conceptually productive."[1] As such, whether small state resources are seen from a quantitative or a qualitative perspective, the ontological questions that they raise,[2] as well as the epistemological questions about the nature of the relationship between the agent and structure, are a function of varying world views.[3] This supports Legro and Moravcsik's argument that paradigmatic developments rely on different auxiliary assumptions that may generate multiple and sometimes "contradictory propositions."[4]

These contradictions are inevitable in the discussion of small state resources given the variations in nation-states across the international system. This is evident in Tom Long's call for "an alternative approach [to small states scholarship] focused on the dynamics of asymmetrical relationship instead of the amorphous category of small (or weak) states, or small (or weak) powers."[5] In these terms, the conceptualization of small states' resources and their relationship to their behavior in the international system can be said to be varied and likely contradictory.[6]

International Relation Theories and Small States' Resources

Power is a key consideration in international relations for vulnerable small states as well as the leading state actors in the system. Defining

---

1   Legro and Moravcsik, "Is Anybody Still a Realist?," 9.
2   Yvonna S. Lincoln and Egon Guba, *Naturalistic Inquiry* (Beverly Hills, CA: Sage Publications, 1985).
3   Rudy Hirschheim and Heinz K. Klein, "Four Paradigms of Information Systems Development," *Communications of the ACM* 32, no. 4 (1989): 1199–1216.
4   Legro and Moravcsik, "Is Anybody Still a Realist?," 9.
5   Tom Long, "It's Not Size, It's the Relationship: From 'Small States' to Asymmetry," *International Politics* 54, no. 2 (2017): 144–160.
6   Jeanne A. K. Hey, "Introducing Small State Foreign Policy," in *Small States in World Politics: Explaining Foreign Policy Behaviour*, ed. J. A. K Hey (Boulder, CO: Lynne Rienner, 2003), 1–12.

power can be challenging and Robert Dahl in his seminal work argues that power is usually defined intuitively and, in such cases, is based around the relationships between people.[1] However, the epistemological contention, as Dahl argues, is distinguishing "association" from "cause." By extending the power-relationship concept so that it includes relationships between people in addition to animate and inanimate objects, Dahl incorporates actors to include "individuals, groups, roles, offices, governments, nation-states or other human aggregates."[2]

For Dahl, the complete conceptualization of power must be framed in terms of the base or sources, the means or the instruments used, the "amount" and "scope" which refer respectively to the extent and the range.[3] While these appear to stem from a realist perspective and have been used as the "basis of realists," Long argues that "it does not inherently favor one type of actor (say, great powers) over others."[4] This helps us to understand state resources in terms of power "in the context of an asymmetric relationship"[5] that uses categorizations such as relational power or weakness[6] or qualitative or quantitative measures of resources.[7] This latter dichotomy provides the context for discussing the resources of small states in relation to international relations theories given that their scope includes both materialistic and non-materialistic attributes.

As long as international affairs continue to be dominated by those countries with the most material power, realist theories will provide a good starting point for any assessment of the resources of small states.

---

1   Robert A. Dahl, "The Concept of Power," *Behavioral Science* 2, no. 3 (1957): 201–215.
2   Ibid.
3   Ibid.
4   Tom Long, "Small States, Great Power? Gaining Influence Through Intrinsic, Derivative, and Collective Power," *International Studies Review* 19, no. 2 (2016): 185–205.
5   Ibid.
6   Matthias Maass, "The Elusive Definition of the Small State," *International Politics* 46, no. 1 (2009): 65–83.
7   Tom Rostoks, "Small States, Power, International Change and the Impact of Uncertainty," in *Small States in Europe: Challenges and Opportunities*, eds. Robert Steinmetz and Anders Wivel (Farnham: Ashgate, 2010), 87–101.

Classic realism which is based on power and size has its origin in Thucydides' *History of the Peloponnesian War*. The resources or bases of power include "military expenditure, size of armed forces, gross national product, size of territory and population."[1] It is on these grounds that traditional or classical realists such as Morgenthau equate the resources of power to "geography, natural resources, industrial capacity, military and population."[2]

In fact, Morgenthau goes further and argues that military power is the most important element of power in international politics.[3] It must, however, be noted that Baldwin indicates that while some realists see power as key, others prioritize the relational aspects of power.[4] The argument, therefore, is that the resources of power are intangible as well as tangible elements. The resources of small states in relation to the realist paradigm can therefore be related to Thorhallsson's categorizations including: fixed size (population), economic size (GDP) or political size (an ability to form a foreign policy consensus).[5] In line with such thinking, small states that lack the necessary resources as defined in realism will, as Vital argues in his influential study, be profoundly vulnerable.[6]

As noted in chapter 1, this realist resource-based view of power continues to be influential in the contemporary era. In their taxonomy of power, Barnet and Duvall define this as compulsory power. However, they differ from traditional thinking about the nexus between power and

---

1 Aigerim Raimzhanova, *Power in IR: Hard, Soft and Smart* (Budapest: Institute for Cultural Diplomacy and the University of Bucharest, 2015).
2 Hans J. Morgenthau, *Politics Among Nations: The Struggle for Power and Peace*, 3rd ed. (Chicago: University of Chicago Press, 1948).
3 Edward H. Carr, *The Twenty Years' Crisis, 1919–1939: An Introduction to the Study of International Relations* (New York: Harper and Row, 1946).
4 David A. Baldwin, "Power and International Relations," in *Handbook of International Relations*, 2nd ed., eds. Walter Carlsnaes, Thomas Risse and Beth A. Simmons (London: Sage Publications, 2012).
5 Baldur Thorhallsson, "Studying Small States: A Review," *Small States & Territories* 1, no. 1 (2018): 17–34.
6 David Vital, *The Inequality of States: A Study of the Small Power in International Relations* (Oxford: Clarendon Press, 1967).

resources by arguing that such compulsory power and the associated resources are not limited to great powers only.[1]

It is also the case that the possession of material resources does not always translate into influence and the ability to change the behaviors of others, which has long been regarded as the essence, and ultimate objective, of power. This supports Long's argument that "power is more complex than compulsion for states of all sizes" and that "a broader interpretation that is more attuned to its structural, institutional and productive aspects suggests additional opportunities for small states."[2] Therefore, in addition to natural resources, other resources—structural, institutional and productive—can also enhance their ability to influence geopolitics. For example, small GCC states with extensive energy resources generate surplus revenues that have been used to create sovereign wealth funds (SWF), that account for at least 40 percent of global SWF assets.[3]

As can be seen in Table 3.1, during the financial crisis of 2008, the small states of the GCC invested heavily in failing or struggling Western financial institutions. This supports Giedrius Cesnakas's argument that "in [the] contemporary international system, energy resources or to be more precise, energy diplomacy becomes an efficient means" of influencing the international system.[4]

---

1   Michael Barnett and Raymond Duvall, "Power in International Politics," *International Organisation* 59, no.1 (2005): 39–75.
2   Long, "Small States, Great Power? Gaining Influence Through Intrinsic, Derivative, and Collective Power," 195.
3   Jeanne Amar, Jean-Francois Carpantier, Christelle Lecourt, *GCC Sovereign Wealth Funds: Why Do They Take, Control*, AMSE Working Papers 1835, Aix-Marseille School of Economics, France.
4   Giedrius Cesnakas, "Energy Resources in Foreign Policy: A Theoretical Approach," *Baltic Journal of Law & Politics* 3, no.1 (2010): 30–52.

Table 3.1. Investments by GCC SWFs in Western Financial Institutions—March 2007– April 2008

SWF	Financial Institution	Investment Value ($ bn)	Holding (%)
Abu Dhabi Investment Authority	Citigroup	7.6	4.9
Saudi Arabia & Singapore Investment Corporation	UBS	10.0	9.0
Borse Dubai	OMX	5.0	**
Kuwait Investment Authority	Citigroup	3.0	1.6
Kuwait Investment Authority	Merrill Lynch	2.0	3.0
Saudi Arabian Monetary Agency	UBS	1.8	2
Mubadala Development Company	The Carlyle Group (US)	1.35	7.5
Qatar Investment Authority	London Stock Exchange	*	24
Qatar Investment Authority	OMX (nordic Stock Exchange, Stockholm)	*	10
Borse Dubai	London Stock Exchange	*	28
Dubai International Capital	OchZiff Capital Management Group (US)	1.1	9.9
Istithmar	Standard Chartered	1.0	2.7
Dubai International Capital	HSBC	1.0	0.4
Qatar Investment Authority	Credit Suisee	0.603	1
Total *(excluding the unknown amounts in the table [*])*		**34.453**	

Notes: * Not specified. ** The amount of shares is yet to be determined pending acceptance of Borse Dubai's offer by OMX shareholders. Borse Dubai, which is owned by three government entities in Dubai, plans to sell its shares in OMX to the US stock exchange, Nasdaq, in a deal that includes both cash and a 20% shareholding in Nasdaq.
Source: Mehmet Asutay, "GCC Sovereign Wealth Funds and Their Role in the European and American Markets," *Equilibri* 12, no. 3 (2008): 335-354.

The above example highlights clearly, albeit only in relation to the GCC energy producers, that small states can enhance their influence in geopolitics through the dispersion of resources in a similar fashion to the system's major powers. However, Legro and Moravcsik emphasize that "realists need only to assume that efficacy is proportional to total material capabilities."[1] This is another way of saying what was clearly stated above: That there are limitations to realism in terms of providing us with a complete foundational understanding of the way that a small state's resources support their capabilities and abilities to influence the international system. The categorization of small states means that those of sufficient (however defined) territorial, political and economic size are able to influence the international political system via a materialistic approach to power even if such influence does not match that of the great powers.

The resources of small states can be considered in liberal as well as a realist terms. Conceptualizing small state resources on the basis of liberalism requires an examination of the key assumptions that underpin this theoretical paradigm. Moravcsik argues that three core assumptions can be advanced about liberalism in international relations theory. The first involves the premise that the "fundamental actors in politics are members of domestic society" including individuals and groups that seek to promote their interests.[2] One implication of this is that politics is situated in a social context that limits the purposes and possibilities of governments and can make politics problematic given that it involves competing, contrasting and contradictory narratives and goals. This explains Berlin's point that "conflict of positive values" makes "social and political collision a necessary part of the political system."[3]

On this basis, liberalism does not automatically produce a convergence of interest and any such convergence is ultimately arrived at under specific conditions. For small states, it is divergent interests of individual claims to

---

1   Legro and Moravcsik, "Is Anybody Still a Realist?," 17.
2   Andrew Moravcsik, "Liberalism and International Relations Theory," Paper No. 92–6, Cambridge, Mass: Centre for European Studies, Harvard University, 1992, 7.
3   Isiah Berlin, "The Pursuit of the Ideal," in *The Crooked Timber of Humanity*, ed. Isiah Berlin (New York: Knopf, 1991), 91.

their rights to life, liberty, territorial integrity, political independence and property, as espoused by John Locke.¹ This provides the basis for the intangible resources of small states in their ability to influence international politics. Michael and Stephano argue that Locke's liberal individualism is the foundation of international law, itself a resource that can be used by small states to ensure their territorial integrity and constrain the actions of great powers.

The second liberal assumption, according to Moravcsik, is that "governments represent some segment of domestic society" and that the interests of this constituency are reflected in the policies of the state.² For a small state, social interests tend to converge around a particular issue such as climate change, women's and minority rights, education and healthcare, accessible public services, and policies that lead to an inclusive society.³ On their own or in combination, all can serve as a currency and a resource that one small state, or several acting together, can use to influence geopolitics.

Such thinking is in line with Beckley's attempt to conceptualize power in terms of outcomes. For example, the North Vietnamese guerrillas can be said to have used their 'resolve' to defeat the United States during the Vietnam War despite the latter's much larger economy, vastly superior military hardware, and the support of powerful international allies. In these terms, for the Vietnamese fighting the US military, national pride and determination were highly valuable resources that supported them in their war against a powerful enemy. It is for this reason that Beckley indicates that intangible traits such as "grit, luck and wisdom (knowledge) also matter, too" as resources of power.⁴

Knowledge is also an important resource that has provided the wherewithal for some small states such as Finland, Estonia, Taiwan and

---

1   Michael Doyle and Stefano Recchia, "Liberalism in International Relations," in *International Encyclopaedia of Political Science*, eds. Bertrand Badie, Dirk-Berg Schlosser and Leonardo Morlina (Los Angeles: Sage, 2011).
2   Moravcsik, "Liberalism and International Relations Theory," 8.
3   Areng, "Lilliputian States in Digital Affairs and Cyber Security," 3.
4   Michael Beckley, "The Power of Nations, Measuring What Matters," *International Security* 43, no. 2 (2018): 7–44.

Ireland to innovate and gain influence in industries such as nanotechnology, biotechnology, telecommunications and cyber security. This has required investment in high quality education, human capital development, research and development and the building of quality institutional frameworks.[1] This underscores another point, that the intangible resources developed by small states can be used in the innovation of new tangible resources. Both state and individual interests can be linked in this endeavor to the third assumption under liberalism—that it encompasses the behavior of the state at the levels of international conflict and cooperation as reflected in the preferences of states. While there are possibilities for divergent preferences, there is also the likelihood of convergent state preferences that lead to cooperation. This cooperation can result in the need for "certain international outcomes" that are external to "specific institutional and geopolitical constraints that are imposed by the international political system" on the availability of such outcomes.[2]

International cooperation can be linked to Thorhallsson's small state categorization of preference size and perceptual size that can themselves be juxtaposed on collective power in relation to small states. Small state preferences on specific issues, for example, as well as their perception of themselves and others' perception of them are likely to provide the basis for relationships between or among small states in addition to other non-superpowers. The purpose of such relationships and collective power is to achieve strength in numbers.[3] Relationships among and between small states are among their resources for international influence. However, as Keohane argues, for these small states to have any significance, they need to be able to work together in large groups and each member of the group must have some minimum influence.[4]

Despite such challenges to their collective and relationship currency or resource, Long provides examples of how small states can use bandwagoning together as a resource that provides them with the opportunity to influence

---

1   Areng, "Lilliputian States in Digital Affairs and Cyber Security," 4–5.
2   Moravcsik, "Liberalism and International Relations Theory," 11.
3   Long, "It's Not Size, It's the Relationship: From 'Small States' to Asymmetry," 150.
4   Robert O. Keohane, "Lilliputians' Dilemmas: Small States in International Politics," *International Organisation* 23, no. 2 (1969): 291–310.

geopolitics. One example offered in chapter 1, is the way that Antigua and Barbuda used thoughtful strategies to win their case against the United States at the WTO. Another example is how organizations in northern Europe led by small states facilitate Scandinavian and Nordic cooperation.[1] Small developing island states have also come together around the issue of climate change, a crisis that threatens their survival, to gain leadership roles in the international system. For example, the *Associated Press* reported in 2018 that small island nations used the opportunity provided to them by the United Nations General Assembly (UNGA), to challenge the climate change denial of then US President Donald J. Trump.[2] According to Benwell, small states have also used "theatrical interventions" and "grandstand tactics" to undermine the decision of the Trump administration to abandon the Paris Climate Change Agreement.[3]

As the above highlights, small states can use democracy, trade and institutions as resources where possible to influence the international system. They also use other soft power resources such as good governance, diplomacy, education, and business and innovation as resources to influence geopolitical issues.[4] For example, the consistently higher performance of small states, including Singapore and Estonia, in the Organization for Economic Cooperation and Development's (OECD) PISA test have shown that smaller state actors can use educational achievement to develop their standing in the world.[5] Another example, one mentioned in the previous chapter, uses the consistent year on year success of the Nordic nations in ranking at the top of the annual Human Development Index (HDI).

---

1 Peter Viggo Jakobsen, "Still Punching above Their Weight? Nordic Cooperation in Peace Operations after the Cold War," *International Peacekeeping* 14, no. 4 (2007): 458–475.

2 Frank Jordans, "Small Islands Use Big Platform to Warn of Climate Change," *Associated Press*, September 28, 2020, https://apnews.com/article/3c4839b3686345a59e3bd009b70bfdc6 (Accessed May 18, 2020).

3 Richard Benwell, "The Canaries in the Coalmine: Small States as Climate Change Champions," *Round Table: The Commonwealth Journal of International Affairs* 100, no. 413 (2011): 199–211.

4 Jonathan McClory, *The New Persuaders II, A 2011 Global Ranking of Soft Power* (London: Institute of Government, 2011).

5 OECD, *PISA – Programme for International Student Assessment*, 2018. www.oecd.org,pisa.

In addition to the realist and liberal traditions, small state resources that support their influence on geopolitical issues can also be seen through an institutionalist prism. This can be contrasted with Thorhallsson's categorization of sovereignty size, perceptual size and preference size given that international institutional development and their functioning affect state sovereignty, national perceptions and preferences. In terms of rational choice institutionalism, which has its origin in institutional economics, specifically from the perspective of transaction cost and agency, it provides resources such as "interdependence, strategic interaction and collective action."[1]

Although these are intangible resources, they are salient to the survival, as well as the standing and influence, of small states in international politics. This is why Thorhallsson notes that "small states scholars generally emphasize the importance of international institutions in the foreign policies of small states."[2] Doing so enables them to achieve favorable outcomes in a challenging world system dominated by the great powers. Katzenstein indicates that small European states have sought to join the EU not only for its various provisions (interdependence, strategic interaction and collective action), but also to restrain the local regional economic hegemon, Germany, from having excessive influence on their domestic affairs.[3] As resources for a small state's geopolitical engagement, strategic interaction and collective actions can also be seen in the Nordic states and their various decisions to join the EU on the basis of economic drivers. Ingebritsen has argued that entry into the EU afforded economic advantages especially in the agricultural (Denmark) and manufacturing (Sweden and Finland) sectors.[4]

---

1   Christer Jonsson and Jonas Tallberg, *Institutional Theory in International Relations* (Lund: Lund University, 2001).
2   Baldur Thorhallsson, "Studying Small States: A Review," *Small States & Territories* 1, no. 1 (2018): 17–34.
3   Peter J. Katzenstein, "The Smaller European States, Germany and Europe," in *Tamed Power: Germany in Europe*, ed. P. J. Katzenstein (Ithaca NY: Cornell University Press, 1997).
4   Christine Ingebritsen, *The Nordic States and European Unity* (Ithaca NY: Cornell University Press, 1998).

A similar assumption can be attributed to historical and normative institutionalism with its emphasis on the use of international organizations to achieve influence and to promote norms and values in international affairs.[1] The existence of international organizations can be a resource for small countries to influence geopolitics, as can be seen in the case of Estonia, a small former Soviet satellite that joined the North Atlantic Treaty Organization (NATO) and the EU, leading to the development of a strong transatlantic relationship. Estonia has combined its excellent education, technological capabilities and membership of NATO and the EU to gain traction in the international system. In recognition of this, in 2008 NATO established its Cooperative Cyber Defence Centre of Excellence in the Estonian capital, Tallinn.[2]

In 1990, to take another example, following its invasion by Iraq, Kuwait used the Arab League and the United Nations as institutional resources to further its international influence. Iraq faced UN sanctions and the diplomatic and military might of a UN-backed 40-strong US-led alliance that expelled it from the small-oil-rich kingdom.[3] International organizations can therefore also serve as resources that provide certain advantages to small states, providing them with protection and helping them achieve their aims within the system.

Normative institutionalism also offers small states important potential resources. The United Nations Charter provided Kuwait, for example, with a resource that it could use to attract the attention of the international community to its plight at the hands of Iraq. This supports Radoman's argument that international laws and norms can be used by small states to further their security and foreign policy objectives. This is very evident in the way small island states that are particularly susceptible to the problem

---

1 Robert W. Cox and Timothy J. Sinclair, *Approaches to World Order* (Cambridge: Cambridge University Press, 1996); Guy B. Peters, *Institutional Theory in Political Science* (London: Pinter, 1999).
2 Areng, "Lilliputian States in Digital Affairs and Cyber Security," 9.
3 George N. Grammas, "Multilateral Responses to the Iraqi Invasion of Kuwait: Economic Sanctions and Emerging Proliferation Controls," *Maryland Journal of International Law* 15, no. 1 (1991): 1-21.

of climate change use international environmental law to achieve international consensus around this grave problem.[1]

In addition to international laws, small states can also use their stable sovereignty as a resource to project their influence on the international stage. On one level, sovereignty is about the authority that is claimed by an institutionalized public authority. Sovereignty can be linked to "diplomacy, international law, warfare and trade regimes"[2] and, as such, institutionalism provides a wide range of intangible resources to small states in their quest to influence the international system.

A fourth international relations theory that can be linked to the intangible resources of small states is constructivism. Dormer argues that at the heart of constructivism lies the "concepts of intersubjectivity, identity or interest, beliefs, norms and agency."[3] The centrality of intersubjectivity to constructivism stems from the assumption that whatever the sum of different state beliefs, it has independent value that is constituted socially as structures.[4] According to Griffiths et al., the emphasis on intersubjectivity in constructivism challenges the realist focus on rational actors, and material constraints as well as the arguments of liberals and institutionalists.[5]

Alexander Wendt, the doyen of constructivist studies, argues on the other hand that intersubjectivity is focused on the construction of identities as well as interest primarily within the system.[6] Therefore, intersubjectivity entails the corrosion of individual state sovereignty in the building of consensus around subjects such as human rights, the prohibition of

---

1 Jelena Radoman, "Small States in World Politics: State of the Art," *Journal of Regional Security* 13, no. 2 (2018): 179–200.
2 Jonsson and Tallberg, *Institutional Theory in International Relations*, 7.
3 Robert Dormer, "The Impact of Constructivism on International Relations Theory: A History," *Kwansei Gakuin University Social Sciences Review* 22, (2017): 51–64.
4 Paul R. Viotti and Mark V. Kaupi, *International Relations Theory* (London: Longman Pearson, 2012).
5 Martin Griffiths, Terry O'Callaghan, Steven C. Roach, *International Relations: The Key Concepts* (New York: Routledge, 2013).
6 Alexander Wendt, "Constructing International Politics," *International Security* 20, no.1 (1995): 71–81.

genocide and transnational arrangements.[1] It can therefore be seen that in Thorhallsson's small state categorization, preference size and perceptual size could be juxtaposed with intersubjectivity, identities and interests in the social realm of constructivism.

This conceptualization provides opportunities for small states to project their individual identities as a resource in support of their efforts to gain influence in the international system. National or state identity can be recognized as such a resource. Campbell and Hall, in seeking to elucidate national identity and the political economy of small states, indicate that regardless of whether a small state is homogeneous or heterogeneous, strong national identity unifies the people as a nation-state.[2] In line with this, they argue that Denmark is an example of a small state with a strong national identity that can be traced back to Lutheranism, a state-sponsored religion that shaped a society defined by self-discipline, high birth-rates and a tendency towards asceticism and egalitarianism.[3]

While this may be something of a generalization, it does highlight the important historical and ideological roots of contemporary national identity. This has, so the argument goes, contributed to Denmark's influence on the international stage and has facilitated institutionalized cooperation, sacrifice, flexibility and state action. Unlike Denmark, which is highly homogeneous, Switzerland is another small state that is heterogeneous but has exploited cultural differences to develop a strong national identity, resulting in strong socioeconomic achievements and notable influence in international banking and finance.[4]

---

1 Robert Dormer, "The Impact of Constructivism on International Relations Theory: A History," *Kwansei Gakuin University Social Science Review* 22, (2017): 51–64.
2 John L. Campbell and John A. Hall, "National Identity and the Political Economy of Small States," *Review of International Political Economy* 16, no. 4 (2009): 547–572.
3 Ibid. See also Sigrun Khal, "The Religious Roots of Modern Poverty Policy: Catholic, Lutheran, and Reformed Protestant Traditions Compared," *Archives of European Sociology* XLVI, no.1 (2005): 91–126.
4 Campbell and Hall, "National Identity and the Political Economy of Small States," 565.

The importance of a distinct national identity as a resource can also be seen in Qatar's hosting of the FIFA World Cup in 2022, as well as other independent policy positions that have created tensions with its fellow GCC members—Saudi Arabia, Bahrain, and the UAE.[1] On one level, Qatar's national identity can also be illuminated by examining scholarly work addressing status-seeking among small states. For example, Wohlforth et al. argue that "small states seek both status among their fellow small states, but also by the great powers." The small states in question do this by taking on admirable tasks or by excelling at a particular task that the international community holds to be valuable. For example, The Netherlands, which hosts the International Criminal Court (ICC) in The Hague, benefits from its international standing as a champion of international law. Switzerland, on the other hand, 'specializes in third party roles, while Norway has developed a reputation as a "do-gooder state."[2] Through their status-seeking resources, small states can also support great powers in the maintenance of the current international order.[3] Status-seeking can also be linked to Thorhallsson's small state categorization with regards to perceptual size and preference size.

The intangible resources of small states can also be related to shelter theory which was "created in an attempt to forecast and explain small state behavior in the international system."[4] This concept will be examined in a subsequent chapter dealing with the security options available to small states, but it is worth noting here that the assumption underpinning shelter theory is that small states have a deficit in realist resources of power such as population, economy, and diplomatic and military capacity. To make up for such deficits, small states "seek political, economic and

---

[1] Thomas Ross Griffin, "National Identity, Social Legacy and Qatar 2022: The Cultural Ramifications of FIFA's First Arab World Cup," *Soccer and Society* 20, no. 7–8 (2019): 1000–1013.

[2] William C. Wohlforth, Benjamin de Carvalho, Halvard Leira and Iver B. Neumann, "Moral Authority and Status in International Relations: Good States and the Social Dimension of Status Seeking," *Review of International Studies* 44, no. 3 (2018): 526–546.

[3] Ibid.

[4] Thorhallsson, "Studying Small States: A Review," 27.

societal shelter provided by larger states and international organizations in order to shield themselves from inbuilt structural weaknesses and a hostile international environment."[1]

The shelter provided by the larger or great power becomes the resource that the small state uses in ensuring that it can influence the international system. Thorhallsson notes that shelter theory, a salient resource in the arsenal of small states, has been used both by Iceland in its international relations as well as the international alliances formed by the Nordic states. In the Middle East it has long been a resource of international influence, especially in the Gulf region where US Central Command (CENTCOM) has bases in Qatar, Bahrain, the UAE and Saudi Arabia, and is responsible for military operations across the region.[2]

National Resources, Power and Small State Foreign Policies

As demonstrated above, small states may have the same resources available to them as great power actors. However, as Vaicekauskaite notes, small states face various challenges that inhibit their abilities to influence the international system through the efficient and effective use of those resources.[3] In order to be able to develop their foreign policies so that they influence the world system, small states must rely on strategic resources that go beyond the traditional sources of power. As the example of Kuwait above highlighted, institutional power factors such as interdependence, as suggested by Keohane and Nye, can be the tool for small states in their attempt to influence the global system.[4] As chapter 5 will address in detail, small states can also use alliances and strategic hedging to increase their influence and achieve security.[5]

The limitations of small states with regards to the traditional resources of power means that they must use their intangible resources

---

1 Ibid.
2 Micah Zenko, *US Military Policy in the Middle East—An Appraisal* (London: Chatham House, 2018).
3 Zivile Marija Vaicekauskaite, "Security Strategies of Small States," *Journal of Baltic Security* 3, no. 2 (2017): 7–15.
4 Barnett and Duvall, "Power in International Politics," 39–75.
5 Marija Vaicekauskaite, "Security Strategies of Small States," 7.

to be able to influence the global system. In addition, small states can also use their self-image developed over time as an intangible resource that increases and consolidates their influence in geopolitics. The image of the Nordic states at the UN in what is referred to as the Nordic UN model has been the product of the commitment of these small countries to peacekeeping, peacebuilding and substantial contributions to international aid disbursements, especially from Denmark, Norway and Sweden.[1] In the *Handbook on the Politics of Small States*, Thorhallsson and Elinardottir argue that in addition to the UN, these Nordic countries have used their economic resources to develop a strong national brand to gain influence on key foreign policy and security issues.[2]

New Zealand is another small state that uses its national image or national branding to project itself in international politics. This has involved differentiating itself from Australia through a branding strategy that includes presenting itself as an Asia-Pacific state in terms of identity. This has given New Zealand influence at the UN as a member of the Economic and Social Commission for Asia and the Pacific.[3] Additionally, New Zealand uses its brand to influence international politics based on cultural attributes built around its indigenous people as well as its prowess in global sports like rugby.[4]

Bahrain, the UAE and Qatar are small Gulf States that have used or are using sports and cultural diplomacy to develop national brands capable of impacting on international politics. The Bahrain and Abu Dhabi Grand Prix are globally influential sporting events. Investment in a wide range of other sporting activities has helped these countries to develop their national images by providing platforms for their influence in global politics. Perhaps most well-known is Qatar's successful bid to host the

---

1 Baldur Thorhallsson and Jóna Sólveig Elínardóttir, "The Nordic States: Keeping Cool at the Top?," in *Handbook on the Politics of Small States*, eds. Godfrey Baldacchino and Anders Wivel (Cheltenham: Edward Elgar Publishing, 2020).
2 Ibid.
3 Tatiana Tokolyova, "Nation- Branding in Small-States Foreign Politics," *Journal of Geography, Politics and Society* 6, no. 4 (2016): 7–14.
4 Ibid.

FIFA 2022 World Cup, which alongside its Al Jazeera satellite TV network has provided traction for Qatar's global status.[1]

This chapter has provided an examination of small states' national resources and the ways that small states can draw on them to increase their international standing and achieve economic and political influence on the world stage. While small states may have access to some of the traditional resources of power that have tended to influence geopolitics, they also face real limitations in these areas when compared to great powers. Yet, the examples provided in this chapter underscore that small states that are willing to adopt an intelligent approach and "take advantage of their flexible, autonomous and informal diplomatic forces,"[2] can successfully use their national resources to project their power in international politics.

---

1   Mohammad Ibahrine, "Nation Branding in the Gulf Countries," in *Intersections Between Public Diplomacy & International Development: Case Studies in Converging Fields*, ed. James Pamment (Los Angeles, CA: Figueroa Press, 2016).

2   Baldur Thorhallsson and Sverrir Steinsson, "Small State Foreign Policy," in *Oxford Research Encyclopaedia of Politics* (2017), 1–25.

CHAPTER 4

Small States as Autonomous Security Actors

There are almost two hundred sovereign states in the world, and they differ in many respects. They have different types of governments and political systems, varying levels of wealth and resources, and contrasting economic and social policies. Yet ensuring security is the basic, non-negotiable task for leaders in every state across the international system. It is also the primary, as well as arguably the oldest, responsibility of the state throughout history.

In many respects, life in the twenty-first century is more secure than ever before. Scientific and technological progress has solved many problems that plagued humankind during previous historical periods. At various levels, including the governmental, we now have more tools to address more problems, including existential challenges to our physical survival, than in the past. Moreover, the end of the Cold War in the late 1980s ameliorated the massive threat of the second half of the twentieth century stemming from a potential escalation of nuclear conflict during the bipolar stand-off between the United States and the Soviet Union.

Nevertheless, we still face numerous long-standing challenges to security, as well as new social, economic, political, and environmental challenges that have emerged over recent decades and target states irrespective of their size. As NATO's website acknowledges, "Today we face a much broader range of threats than in the past."[1] Dealing with these diverse security issues is extremely challenging for states both big and small. One can argue, however, that larger states have a better basis for

---

1 "What are today's security challenges," # WEARENATO (Accessed May 10, 2020) https://www.nato.int/wearenato/security-challenges.html.

developing effective security policies in response to these wide-ranging challenges due to various size-related factors, most notably a greater level of surplus capabilities. It is assumed, at the same time, that smaller states generally have fewer economic, financial, demographic, defense and other material resources than bigger ones. This reality can limit the security infrastructure available to small states, not simply in their capacity to wage war but also their capacity to engage in diplomacy and other non-violent means of international engagement.[1]

For this reason, size can be an important factor not only in determining state influence but also the extent to which, as Reid and others have argued, a state can play a role in consolidating its own security in the international system.[2] This explains why small state theorists like Jervis, who was quoted in chapter 1, consider the external environment to be a much more important variable for a small state than it is for a major state actor.[3] Linked to this, the consensus view in the literature is that small states find it hard to provide for their own security because they lack defensive capacity and rarely succeed in achieving their own offensive strategic goals in response to the geopolitical and other security risks that they face. This creates a vulnerability that is widely presented as the most striking consequence of smallness in security affairs.

This does not change the fact that all small states have a fundamental binary choice in security terms. They can align with other actors in the system (including other states) to achieve security or they can attempt to maintain security autonomously. The traditional assumption in the literature is that small states that embrace autonomous security policies will be more vulnerable and lack relative influence compared to those that prioritize

---

[1] Diana Panke, "Studying Small States in International Security Affairs: A Quantitative Analysis," *Cambridge Review of International Affairs* 30, no. 2–3 (2017): 235–255.

[2] G. L. Reid, *The Impact of Very Small Size on the International Relations Behavior of Microstates* (London: Sage, 1974).

[3] Robert Jervis, "Cooperation Under the Security Dilemma," *World Politics* 30, no.2 (1978): 167–214. See also James N. Rosenau, *Turbulence in World Politics: A Theory of Change and Continuity* (Princeton, New Jersey: Princeton University Press, 1990).

cooperation or alignment primarily in the form of alliances. As Rickli succinctly put it, small states "can either opt for influence or autonomy."[1]

If a small state does look to maximize its influence by opting for alliances over autonomy it can gain some advantages, notably protection. As alliances can never be taken for granted, this choice can also increase the small state's risk of both entrapment and abandonment.[2] One notable example is the 2006 decision of the United States to close its Naval Air Station at Keflavik in Iceland after fifty years of operational activity. Over the previous half century, this US base, which was the size of a small town and home to five thousand troops, was on the front-line of the Cold War. It was closed against the wishes of the Icelandic government, and almost immediately following the US departure Iceland experienced a rise in Russian assertiveness and encroachment.[3]

This chapter begins by introducing the concept of security and the ways that thinking about it have evolved in international affairs. In doing so, it addresses notions of security that are particularly impactful for small states. These include those that transcend the traditional, state-centered view, and which are increasingly key considerations in international affairs. Among the most important are environmental, food and other forms of human security, a term that is now widely established in the academic literature and used by practitioners working in major organizations like the UN to describe the real-world challenges that they face.

This chapter then presents some key sources of insecurity that preoccupy thinkers and policy-makers dealing with more recent, as well

---

1   Hans Mouritzen, *External Danger and Democracy: Old Nordic Lessons and New European Challenges* (Aldershot, UK: Ashgate, 1997), 101–106; Anders Wivel, "The Security Challenge of Small EU Member States: Interests, Identity and the Development of the EU as a Security Actor," *Journal of Common Market Studies* 43, no. 2 (2005): 393–412.
2   Hakan Wiberg, "Security Problems of Small Nations," in *Small States and the Security Challenge in the New Europe*, eds. Werner Bauwens, Armand Clesse and Olav Knudsen (London: Brassey's, 1996), 21–41.
3   Gregory Winger and Gustav Peterson, "Return to Keflavik Station," *Foreign Affairs*, February 24, 2016. https://www.foreignaffairs.com/articles/united-states/2016-02-24/return-keflavik-station.

as older and more established, forms of threats. In doing so, it is intended to highlight the importance of threat perceptions for how security policies are developed in small states. This is particularly relevant to any study of small state security because a state's perception of its environment, as well as its willingness to take any given course of action, are often as important as the environment itself.[1] The final part of this chapter examines the approaches and strategies that small states can adopt to address the threats and security challenges that they face. This analysis will be considered primarily in terms of the small state's quest for autonomous security. The vitally important role of alliances in the security of small states will be addressed fully in the next chapter.

Negotiating Autonomy in the Small State

For small states to gain security from alignment and alliances, they require assurances or practical support from more powerful partners. Autonomous security, on the other hand, places the emphasis on the resources and power bases that small states may possess individually, independent of potential or actual partners or allies. Those resources are often, most obviously and in some circumstances most importantly, found in a nation's military and defense sectors. This highlights a significant difficulty faced by small states that want to provide for their own security in isolation: they tend to rank lower than larger ones in all measures of military power. This is clear when one examines military spending as a share of GDP, a traditionally important though by no means decisive indicator of military power. An examination of 2018 figures shows that there are only very few small states among the top 40 countries.

---

1   See M. Papadakis and H. Starr, "Opportunity, Willingness, and Small States: The Relationship Between Environment and Foreign Policy," in *New Directions in the Study of Foreign Policy*, eds. C. F. Hermann, C. W. Kegley, J. Rosenau (Boston: Allen & Unwin, 1987), 409–432.

Table 4.1. Top 40 Military Spenders in 2018, Including as Share of GDP

Country	Rank in top 40 military spenders	Military Expenditure 2018, (Spending in billon $US)	Spending as share of GDP (%)
For comparison: USA	(1)	649	3.2
Saudi Arabia	(3)	[67.6] SIPRI estimate	[8.8]
*United Arab Emirates (UAE)	(14) in 2014	22.8 in 2014	5.6 in 2014 (2018 unavailable)
Israel	(17)	15.9	4.3
Singapore	(22)	10.8	3.1
Taiwan	(23)	10.7	1.8
Kuwait	(27)	7.3	5.1
Norway	(28)	7.1	1.6
Oman	(30)	[6.7] SIPRI estimate	[8.2]
Sweden	(33)	5.8	1.0
Belgium	(37)	5.0	0.9
Switzerland	(38)	4.8	0.7

Source: Adapted from "Trends in World Military Expenditure, 2018," *SIPRI Fact Sheet*, April 2019, https://sipri.org/sites/default/files/2019-04/fs_1904_milex_2018_0.pdf, p. 2; UAE data from Pieter D. Wezeman and Alexandra Kuimova, "Military Spending and Arms Imports by Iran, Saudi Arabia, Qatar and the UAE," *SIPRI Fact Sheet*, May 2019, https://www.sipri.org/sites/default/files/2019-05/fs_1905_gulf_milex_and_arms_transfers.pdf, p. 6.

This underscores the fact that the military and defense sectors of most small states are either underdeveloped or at the very least lag behind larger powers in terms of their capabilities. There are multiple reasons as to why this is the case. Apart from a lack of economic and financial resources, in demographic terms small states have a smaller population to recruit into specialized, as well as larger conventional, military units. Beyond measures of nominal military power, including spending, the size of the recruitment pool and the size of a state's military apparatus, the potential for deterrence and self-defense rests on security capabilities in the wider sense.[1]

---

1 Ivan Arreguin-Toft, "How the Weak Win Wars: A Theory of Asymmetric Conflict," *International Security* 26, no. 1 (2001): 93–128.

These include, for instance, strategically located bases like those controlled by the UAE in Eritrea and Somaliland; and specific areas of absolute military strength such as Estonia's status as a global leader in cyber security. There can be circumstances in which military threats do not necessarily require a military response but rather different types of instruments of national power in order to achieve economic or political solutions and outcomes. On these occasions, small states can draw on non-military resources to achieve security at home as well as influence abroad. These resources include governmental stability and strong domestic institutions, science and technology and, as demonstrated in chapters 2 and 3, other national and natural resources, such as energy supplies. All of this recognizes the fact that small states do, and indeed should, employ indirect security strategies intended to foster conditions in the regional or international systems that are favorable to their national interests and security needs.

International Relations (IR) scholars tend to work with a definition of security that involves the "alleviation of threats to cherished values."[1] This raises one immediate and fundamental question—whose security are we talking about when we talk about security? In principle, it could be the security of the existing regime or government, or a specific national asset (like an oil or gas sector), or a particular ethnic or national group, or even the security of the environment. Though all are relevant to this study, traditionally the answer has been that security refers to the security of the state itself and relates directly to the concept of national security—the actual protection of the sovereign state from internal and external threats.

Territorial size is relevant for a state's security on these grounds because, as International Relations scholars have long highlighted, and as the US invasion of Panama in late 1989 and the Iraqi invasion of Kuwait in 1990 demonstrated, in conventional wars countries with small territories can be overrun within hours. At the same time, territorial size as it relates to security can be a relative concept. For example, Finland is

---

1   Paul D. Williams and Matt McDonald, "An Introduction to Security Studies," in *Security Studies: An Introduction*, eds. P. D. Williams and M. McDonald (London/New York: Routledge, 2018), 1–13.

not a small country on the basis of its land mass but its small population, limited military power, and location next to Russia makes it a vulnerable small state in territorial terms.[1] Small states can also have different geographical characteristics. For example, landlocked small states and small island states face unique security challenges from traditional and non-traditional threats.

For much of its modern history, Switzerland practiced defensive neutrality as a way of dealing with its status as a landlocked small state surrounded by much larger powers, notably Germany and France. This placed a heavy emphasis on the isolationist aspect of neutrality. In other words, Switzerland stayed out of world affairs for the sake of its own protection. Importantly, this strategy enabled Switzerland to survive the Second World War unscathed and left it in control of its sovereignty over the entire course of the Cold War. This is a reminder that if a small state chooses autonomy over alignment then it will most likely adopt neutrality as part of a defensive policy in order to protect its sovereignty from stronger actors in the system.[2]

In its modern form, the legal definition of neutrality introduced in the Hague Convention of 1907, ruled out alliance participation as it required a neutral sovereign state to "abstain from war directly and indirectly." In 1948, Finland, for example, signed a Treaty of Friendship, Cooperation and Mutual Assistance (FCMA) with the Soviet Union. Under the terms of this agreement, Moscow required Finland to embrace a policy of "passive neutrality" and avoid involvement in Western alliances including politico-economic ones like the Marshall Plan, as well as military ones like the newly-established NATO.[3] The foreign policy behavior embodied in this Finnish approach even led to the adoption of the term

---

1 Christopher S. Browning, "Small, Smart and Salient? Rethinking Identity in the Small States Literature," *Cambridge Review of International Affairs* 19, no. 4 (2006): 669–684.
2 J. M. Rickli, "European Small States' Military Policies After the Cold War: From Territorial to Niche Strategies," *Cambridge Review of International Affairs* 21, no.3 (2008): 307–325.
3 Browning, "Small, Smart and Salient? Rethinking Identity in the Small States Literature," 676.

"Finlandization", to describe how a small state located beside a great power attempts to maximize security on the defensive level.[1]

Old Threats, New Threats and Threat Perceptions

Traditional national security concerns have been of central importance across decades of security debates and policy implementation. It is also the case that the exclusive focus on national security at the expense of other softer security considerations is becoming more and more outdated. One can even argue that it was always insufficient given its sole focus on the security of the state. In reality, nearly all aspects of security transcend national boundaries. This is true for threats as well as effective responses to threats, which mostly consist of a variety of alliance options that will be addressed in the next chapter and which, by their very nature, are extraterritorial on all levels. Such threats include those that are a direct and immediate result of deliberate human action, such as terrorism and transnational organized crime, both of which are not new but preoccupy security thinking in the globalized era to an unprecedented extent.

There are also threats which are also wholly or at least partly the result of human action or inaction, but whose causes are more complex, and whose effects are of a larger scale. These include environmental risks, health pandemics, like the Coronavirus (COVID-19) crisis of 2020–21, and regional and global financial crises like those that occurred across the international system between 2008 and 2010. All have contributed to our widening understanding of threat perceptions in recent decades. They have also contributed to the rising acceptance of the view that effective security responses require transnational solutions.

During the Cold War, many experts on global politics and security, including those involved in the academic discipline of Security Studies, almost exclusively focused on traditional state-based threats, especially conventional war. Since the end of the Cold War, the conceptualization of security has become more differentiated and multifarious. Phrases such as "new security challenges" or "the new security agenda" highlight the

---

1   Hans Mouritzen, "Small States and Finlandisation in the Age of Trump," *Survival* 59, no. 2 (2017): 67–84.

inclusion of potential and actual threats formerly deemed part of the realm of low politics. These include environmental degradation and climate change, risks to health security, underdevelopment and poverty, and food and water insecurity.

Not everyone agrees that it is appropriate to include such problems under the heading of security, because in most cases they do not pose an immediate or grave danger to life at the same level as large-scale armed conflict. Strategic planners with a strong focus on the military may, for example, argue that one cannot treat a specific issue as a security threat if "the use of force, or even the logistical or technical assistance that can be supplied by military units does little to respond to a given problem."[1] In similar terms, and with respect to environmental issues, some authors are willing to include them in discussions on security only to the extent that they are a cause of conflict. They are less willing to consider them as intrinsic security threats in their own right so as not to dilute the traditional notion of security.[2]

It is true that when it comes to new threats, especially those that are not the direct and immediate result of the application of violence through human action (like war or terrorism), there are limits to what military planning or strategy can do. For instance, there are no military solutions to the impact of climate change—quite the contrary, considering the carbon footprint and other environmental impacts of defense industries and war. Most of the literature, however, would argue that new threats are most definitely to be included within the boundaries of security.

Political theorists have long argued that peace is more than just the absence of war and scholars have made a similar point about security on the grounds that "being secure means more than being free of any immediate risk of death." This, it is argued, is due to the fact that "some of

---

1 James J. Wirtz, "A new agenda for Security and Strategy?" in *Strategy in the Contemporary World*, 5th ed., eds. John Baylis et al. (Oxford: Oxford University Press, 2016), 337–354.

2 Daniel H. Deudney, "Environmental Security: A Critique," in *Contested Grounds: Security and Conflict in the New Environmental Politics*, eds. Daniel H. Deudney and Richard A. Matthew (Albany: State University of New York Press, 1999), 187–222.

life's most significant insecurities arise not at the barrel of a gun, but in the invisible and insidious capillaries of power that condition and shape the possibilities and potentialities of life itself."[1]

Whatever view one holds on the above debate, it is empirically demonstrable that in numerical terms many more people are killed or exposed to severe risk to physical, material, and psychological safety by non-traditional threats than through conventional wars. Their impacts are far more pervasive and include a host of potential and sometimes unknown cascade effects. Non-traditional threats are also transnational and interdependent in so much as the environment, food and water, the economy, and national and international development are all interconnected. This can result in a domino or negative trickle-down effect across the entire system because these threats, as the COVID-19 pandemic underscored, do not stop at the borders of states, whether they are rich or poor, small or large.

None of the so-called new threats that have long-term, severe impacts are technically new. Climate change, environmental and energy insecurity, food and water insecurity, and health crises have always endangered people, both individually and collectively. Negative effects of environmental degradation and food insecurity have always existed, and so have epidemics and pandemics. However, all are part of the more recent trend of thinking about human security in general in the same ways as hard power threats were traditionally perceived.[2]

As highlighted repeatedly in this book, there are many different types of small states. This demands that generalizations be made with caution. However, it is possible to say that at least in regards to climate change, food insecurity, epidemics and pandemics, states with small territories and small populations are more likely to experience their severe impacts. Small states can be particularly vulnerable regarding the access,

---

1 Lee Jarvis and Jack Holland, *Security: A Critical Introduction* (New York: Palgrave Macmillan, 2014), 152.
2 Mai Yamani, "Health, Education, Gender and Security of the GCC in the Twenty-first Century," in *Gulf Security in the Twenty-First Century*, eds. David E. Long and Christian Koch (Abu Dhabi: The Emirates Centre for Strategic Studies and Research, 1997).

availability, utilization and stability of food supplies due to limited land availability, susceptibility to natural disasters, deep integration into global markets (in the case of dependency on imports) and, in many cases, insularity and isolation, as is evident in the experience of Small Island Developing States (SIDS).

From the perspective of human security, food security is an issue because the adequate provision of nutritious food is a fundamental responsibility of the state and is also considered to be, along with access to clean water, a universal human right in a number of important international agreements signed since the end of the Second World War.[1] Although progress was made during the latter decades of the twentieth century to combat hunger, it has been estimated that as recently as 2009 one billion people were malnourished. When nutrient-deficient diets were included in the calculations on food access, that number rose to around two billion, just under a third of the world's population.[2] By 2019, it was estimated that the number of malnourished people in the world had increased further, due primarily to the impact of economic slowdowns, climate change, and a surge in the number and complexity of conflicts in Africa and the Near East.[3]

Even if we do not adopt a human security perspective, it is still evident that there are multiple connections between food and other dimensions of security. Food insecurity, for example, impacts negatively on the health and well-being of communities. As shall be seen below in relation to Small Island Developing States (SIDS) in the Pacific region, inadequate access to nutrition impacts the health sector, for instance through large-scale occurrence of non-communicable diseases and poor diets. Food insecurity can also destabilize domestic politics and can lead to competition and conflict for

---

1   UN Declaration on Human Rights (1948); International Covenant on Economic, Social and Cultural Rights (1966); Declaration to end Hunger and Malnutrition (1974); World Food Summit pledge (1996); and the Food Assistance Convention (2012).
2   Jarvis and Holland, *Security: A Critical Introduction*, 157.
3   Food and Agriculture Organization of the United Nations (FAO), *Help Eliminate Hunger and Malnutrition*, Rome: FAO, 2019, 1. http://www.fao.org/3/ca3923en/ca3923en.pdf.

access to resources. Linked to this, food supply, which is vital for survival and must be secured continuously, becomes vulnerable to a whole array of political factors in the short term unlike those raw materials needed for manufacturing and the running of heavy industries, which only result in economic losses in the case of shortages.

There is also a significant link between food security and global climate change as the latter makes the challenge of producing adequate levels of food more difficult.[1] Environmental degradation through collective human activity has been occurring at least since the Industrial Revolution—though it has differed in form and scope from region to region. It is, however, only in the final decades of the twentieth century, and especially since the beginning of the twenty-first century, that the long-term consequences of human manipulation of the Earth's ecosystems has garnered global attention. It is possible that even in this current century, the high rates of global greenhouse gas (GHG) emissions could result in temperature levels and humidity that exceed the body's ability to cool down through perspiration. In that scenario, being outdoors could lead to a severe risk to health and even be life-threatening.[2] This has numerous implications for economic security as well as for the spreading of vector borne diseases, terrestrial and marine ecosystems, the availability of fresh water, agriculture and energy systems.

According to a widely cited paper from the journal *Nature Communications* that relies on an artificial intelligence device (CoastalDEM) that corrects error rates from previous data, sea levels are projected to rise between 20–30 centimeters by the middle of the twenty-first century. The potential consequences of this include the complete disappearance of at least a dozen cities worldwide; average annual coastal floods that could affect more than three hundred million people; and high

---

[1] John Connell and Kristen Lowitt, eds. *Food Security in Small Island States* (Singapore: Springer Nature, 2020), v.

[2] Jeremy S. Pal and Elfatih A. B. Eltahir, "Future Temperature in Southwest Asia Projected to Exceed a Threshold for Human Adaptability," *Nature Climate Change* 6, no. 2 (February 2016): 197–200; Jim Krane, "Climate Action Versus Inaction: Balancing the Costs for Gulf Energy Exporters," *British Journal of Middle Eastern Studies* 47, no. 1 (2020): 117–135.

tides that could permanently rise above land currently occupied by over one hundred and fifty million people.[1] This threat is by no means limited to small states. The government of Indonesia, the world's most populous Muslim country, is now planning to move its capital from Jakarta, a coastal city, to Borneo where it has plans to create a green city from scratch.[2]

The World Health Organization (WHO) classifies fifty-eight countries as Small Island Developing States (SIDS).[3] States included in this category are especially vulnerable to climate change impacts such as extreme weather events, rising sea levels, and stressed water resources due in part to their extensive coastlines in relation to land.[4] Those SIDS with a significant share of their population in coastal areas less than 10 meters above sea level are even more vulnerable to rising sea levels and storm surges. Under a variety of scenarios, states including the Maldives, Marshall Islands and Tuvalu are likely to become uninhabitable before the end of this century.

In nineteenth century Europe, there was a strong awareness of the need to cooperate internationally in order to stem the spread of infectious diseases. The period after the Second World War saw considerable progress in this area. By the mid-twentieth century, infectious diseases were not seen as a vital issue in the West as several viruses, such as smallpox, were eradicated, though they continued to be a health problem in the developing world. For this reason, during the second half of the twentieth century up to the end of the Cold War, health vulnerabilities

---

1 Scott A. Kulp and Benjamin H. Strauss, "New Elevation Data Triple Estimates of Global Vulnerability to Sea-Level Rise and Coastal Flooding," *Nature Communications* 10, no. 4844 (2019): 1–12.

2 Mayuri Mei Lin and Rafki Hidayat, "Jakarta, the Fastest-Sinking City in the World," *BBC News*, August 13, 2018. https://www.bbc.com/news/world-asia-44636934. See also Rebecca Henschke and Abraham Utama, "When Your Capital is Sinking…Start Again?," *BBC News*, March 5, 2020 (Accessed May 20, 2020) https://www.bbc.co.uk/news/extra/xsyGF2fhsL/Indonesia_new_capital.

3 'Special Initiative on Climate Change and Health in Small Island Developing States," World Health Organization, 2011. https://www.who.int/news/item/06-11-2017-special-initiative-on-climate-change-and-health-in-small-island-developing-states.

4 John Connell and Kristen Lowitt, eds. *Food Security in Small Island States* (Singapore: Springer Nature, 2020), 3.

were mostly associated with underdevelopment not with security.

Starting from the 1990s, the exclusive association between health and development was reversed and pandemics began to appear on national security agendas of states and international institutions around the world. Growing concerns over these "more diffuse risks"[1] were influenced by the spread of HIV/AIDS in the 1980s alongside other infectious diseases. There were also growing concerns over bioterrorism in the post-Cold War world. By the start of the current century even national intelligence agencies such as the US Central Intelligence Agency (CIA) had begun to acknowledge communicable diseases as an issue of national security, in the same way that they had long considered nuclear weapons and terrorism.

The 2020 COVID-19 pandemic demonstrates vividly the extent to which these issues can flare up and take on much bigger dimensions, climbing up the priority ladder from low to high security concerns. During 2020, no topic dominated the international headlines more than the COVID-19 outbreak, spreading initially from Wuhan, China, to various countries in Asia, Europe, the Americas and the rest of the world. This case exemplifies in an unprecedented manner the links between health and various dimensions of security, which have come to be increasingly acknowledged by experts and policymakers in recent decades.

Within a few months of COVID-19 being identified, it had taken a severe toll on even large, developed nations, such as Italy, Germany and the United States. In addition to the human cost, it has caused extensive economic disruption that can also result in a massive security impact for both those states worst hit and the wider global economy. As early in the crisis as April 2020, the WTO already predicted that the fallout of the virus would cause the worst global recession of our lifetimes.[2] By

---

1 Colin McInnes, "Health," in *Security Studies: An Introduction*, eds. Paul D. Williams and Matt McDonald (London, New York: Routledge, 2018), 541–555.
2 Zachary Evans, "World Trade Organization Head Warns of Deepest Recession 'Of Our Lifetimes' in Wake of Coronavirus Pandemic," *National Review*, April 8, 2020 (Accessed May 20, 2020) https://www.nationalreview.com/news/world-trade-organization-head-warns-of-deepest-recession-of-our-lifetimes-in-wake-of-coronavirus-pandemic/.

mid-summer 2020, the IMF had predicted that the global economy would shrink by 3 percent over the course of the year, and described COVID-19 as a "crisis like no other," responsible for the worst economic decline since the Great Depression of the 1930s.[1]

Such a challenge in the form of an epidemic or pandemic can be very bad for a large developed state as the American experience demonstrated during 2020 and the first half of 2021. But for a small state with weak infrastructure and limited resources it can prove disastrous. An outbreak of a large-scale communicable disease in a country with a small population has potentially severe consequences for all economic sectors and can contribute to economic decline in several ways. Notably, it can force increased government spending on health or the economy as a whole and see rapidly rising health insurance costs. It can reduce productivity through increased worker absenteeism.

This is particularly problematic in states with small populations if people with key skills fall victim to the disease over the longer-term. It can also lead to reduced levels of internal and external investment due to a lack of business confidence and a fall in demand for natural resources such as oil and gas due to lower production and consumption levels across the global economic system. This was evident in 2002–03 during the short-lived SARS outbreak. It resulted in fewer than a thousand deaths, but its cost in terms of lost trade and investment was estimated to run into the tens of billions of dollars.

It has also been suggested, though not confirmed, that major international actors like the United States and United Kingdom attempted to pressurize the WHO into not declaring the swine flu a pandemic in 2009 due to concerns over the negative economic consequences of such a move on the international economy at a time of widespread financial crisis.[2] Beyond economic damage, pandemics can cause, in worst case scenarios, social disruption and also threaten the effective functioning of a state. In small

---

1 Lora Jones, Daniele Palumbo and David Brown, "Coronavirus: A visual guide to the economic impact," *BBC News,* June 29, 2020 (Accessed July 13, 2020) https://www.bbc.com/news/business-51706225#:~:text=Many%20people%20have%20lost%20their,major%20economies%20as%20a%20result.
2 McInnes, "Health," 548.

states, strains on public sectors, which are often large in comparison with the size of the country, can be so severe that the provision of normal public services can falter both during and after the immediate health crisis.

Small states can also be particularly susceptible to the negative impact of more low-level health crises. SIDS in the Pacific region have some of the worst rates of non-communicable diseases with the burden falling most on the smaller SIDS like the Cook Islands, Nauru and Niue, that are home to less than 20,000 people and exhibit much higher per-capita rates of obesity, diabetes and raised levels of blood pressure among inhabitants than the international average.[1]

In these cases, size and geographical features in particular present profound challenges for key economic sectors such as food and agriculture and often mean that small states are dependent on imports for basic supplies. Difficulties and imbalances in these sectors can, in turn, impact on the national health and long-term vulnerability of populations across many areas of endeavor. While the dynamics outlined above do not necessarily have immediate consequences for small state security, in overall terms they invariably increase vulnerability and dependence. It is also the case that logistical difficulties in some sectors, especially related to the import of medical and pharmaceutical products, not only entrench dependence but can have a more direct link to security in the wider sense, if it makes access to vaccines for infectious diseases harder to ensure. The challenges of non-communicable diseases addressed above are not necessarily included in our common understanding of security threats, as infectious diseases would be. They do, however, highlight the interconnectedness between small state security and non-traditional threats.

Small States and the Limits of Autonomy

In previous chapters it has been argued that smallness is not necessarily a decisive, or even at times a relevant, factor in explaining a state's foreign policy behavior and influence in the international system. A small country

---

1 S. Tu'akoi, M. Vickers, K. Tairea, Y. Aung, N. Tamarua-Herman, M. 'Ofanoa and J. Bay, "The Significance of DOHaD for Small Island Developing States," *Journal of Developmental Origins of Health and Disease* 9, no. 5 (2018): 487–491.

can pursue a successful foreign and security policy. It can use soft power and "enlarge virtually," as Chong has termed it, or use its economic strength and national resources to increase international standing, and forge cooperative trade and security alliances with larger states.[1]

It is also the case that although non-traditional threats affect all countries, large and small, for small countries the risks associated with food and water insecurity, environmental degradation, climate change, and health crises, are augmented and multiplied. In the context of these threats, a small population and/or a small territory do matter. Threats such as pandemics cannot be warded off through effective soft-power instruments or diplomacy or alliance-building. There are also limits to what the military of a small state, no matter how effective, can do to ameliorate the impact of food or water insecurity or climate change, to name three examples.

The measures that small states can, and must, take to be able to respond to non-traditional threats are at the domestic level and include, above all, developing effective, flexible and resilient governance capabilities. In order to do so, small states need to take heed of the findings of research into social-ecological systems around the world. This argues that decentralized governance structures are vital if states want to be able to enhance adaptive capacity to meet the "challenges of global change." The key point here is that decentralized governance structures enable small states to "engage a range of actors and organizations at different scales." This in turn can foster three capabilities that are required to strengthen resilience in the face of a host of non-traditional threats in ways that are vital to long-term security—"flexibility, diversity and social learning."[2]

Decentralized governance may not be possible in all contexts for a variety of reasons. Small states are usually centrally organized due to the small size of their territories and populations. Nevertheless, there is still a

---

1 Alan Chong, "Small State Soft Power Strategies: Virtual Enlargement in the Cases of the Vatican City State and Singapore," *Cambridge Review of International Affairs* 23, no. 3 (2010): 383–405.

2 Kristen Lowitt, Arlette Saint Ville, Patsy Lewis, and Gordon M. Hickey, "Environmental Change and Food Security: The Special Case of Small Island Developing States," *Regional Environmental Change* 15, (2015):1293–1298.

lesson for countries with a strong, central government: The recruitment and inclusion of various stakeholders into processes of adaptive capacity building and projects (national or sub-national) for building resilience in socio-ecological and economic terms is better than attempts by central governments to find solutions all alone.

While in no way underplaying the threat posed to small states by non-traditional threats, classic notions of national security are still relevant and may even be of increasing relevance due to the reemergence of aspiring regional and global hegemons. This is complicated somewhat by the fact that even traditional actors with expansionist or revisionist goals are increasingly adopting hybrid capabilities to achieve their strategic objectives. These methods include the use of non-military and military measures, as well as overt and covert means, including disinformation, cyber-attacks, economic pressure, deployment of irregular armed groups and use of proxy forces. Hybrid methods will usually remain "below the threshold of formally declared warfare," but as a NATO report on hybrid threats has summed up, these coercive and subversive efforts are highly effective in the ways that they can "blur the lines between war and peace, and attempt to sow doubt in the minds of target populations. The speed, scale and intensity of hybrid threats have increased in recent years."[1]

The vulnerabilities created by hybrid threats provide a reminder as to why decision-makers in small states tend to prioritize autonomous approaches to security that avoid the detrimental outcomes of escalation, especially war. Thus, when we discuss strategic choices in this chapter, we mean deliberate approaches to ensuring safety from threats to cherished values (the definition of security we adopt in this study). That said, there are interesting cases of weak party escalation—scenarios where escalation was and is a rational choice for a weaker state or smaller party.

Angstrom and Petersson identify four such scenarios in which a smaller state actor will escalate a crisis in order (1) to provoke a desired over-reaction from the stronger adversary that can be beneficial for the smaller and weaker party as it may trigger outside help; (2) to enable the

---

1   "NATO's response to hybrid threats," NATO, August 8, 2019 (Accessed May 21, 2020) https://www.nato.int/cps/en/natohq/topics_156338.htm.

compartmentalization of conflict within a domain in which the small state can, despite its overall inferiority, maintain escalatory dominance; (3) to create a division of labor with a stronger ally, whereby the small state's contribution may raise its risk on one level but, on the macro-level, may provide it with shelter behind the capabilities of the stronger partner; (4) to forge a reputation of not yielding lightly in order that in the future other actors will think twice before using coercion or the threat of coercion against it.

These four possible scenarios suggest that even if the immediate consequences of escalation are negative for a small state facing a stronger opponent, the "long-run benefits of maintaining a reputation of being steadfast can be more important."[1] However, the authors also point out that weak party escalation is empirically very rare (it does not happen very often) and, it is only a rational choice for a small and weaker actor if one or more of the conditions outlined in the four above scenarios are met.[2]

The Swiss case, briefly mentioned above, illuminates a number of lessons for small states in terms of the options available once defensive neutrality is chosen as the primary way to achieve autonomous security. When the Cold War ended, Switzerland embraced a much more "proactive engagement in the world" by undertaking a policy of "peace promotion."[3] Over time, this led to the institutionalization of "civilian peacebuilding" as a key foreign policy priority. As noted in a report on the new Swiss Foreign Policy Strategy introduced in 1993, this move was a rejection of the isolationist interpretation of neutrality in favor of "international cooperation and participation in international decision-making bodies" as the two guiding principles of Swiss foreign policy.[4] "A passive understanding of neutrality has become obsolete," explained then Swiss foreign minister Micheline Calmy-Rey. "Today, Switzerland can and

---

1. Jan Angstrom and Magnus Petersson "Weak Party Escalation: An Underestimated Strategy for Small States?," *Journal of Strategic Studies* 42, no. 2 (2019): 282–300.
2. Ibid.
3. Andreas Graf and David Lanz, "Switzerland as a Paradigmatic Case of Small-State Peace Policy?," *Swiss Political Science Review* 19, no. 3 (2013): 410–423.
4. Ibid.

must conduct an active policy of neutrality .... And an active policy of neutrality requires different foreign policy instruments, for example, an engaged peace policy."[1]

In the more than a quarter of a century since Switzerland adopted this significant change, it has developed an impressive reputation as a key international mediator and a well-known neutral participant in foreign affairs. In recent years, for example, the country has represented US interests in Iran and Cuba and, after 2008, served as an intermediary between Russia and Georgia in their ongoing conflict. In these terms, active neutrality has considerably extended Swiss influence in international affairs, disproportionate to its size and in spite of its history of restraint in exercising power. At the same time, this new activism has not in any way reduced or diluted Switzerland's capacity for self-reliance in providing for its own security.

This underscores the point that for small states there are different types of neutrality that can be chosen on the basis of different rationales. In line with this thinking, neutrality in its passive/isolationist form can contribute decisively to small state survival in high-level conflict contexts, like those faced by Switzerland during the Second World War and the Cold War. However, as the security environment changes on the global or regional levels, small states may attempt to rethink their positions on neutrality and move from isolationist neutrality to active neutrality in response to emerging risks and opportunities.

It is also the case that non-alignment in the form of neutrality does not necessarily represent a strategic choice. Rather, in its initial conception non-alignment was the institutionalized form of an ideological stance promoted at the 1955 Bandung conference by relatively significant regional leaders including Yugoslavia's Tito, Egypt's Nasser, India's Nehru and Indonesia's Sukarno. In turn, this ideology formed the intellectual framework for the establishment of the Non-Aligned Movement in Belgrade in 1961, with its goal of moving away from great-power interests towards developmental questions, the issue of global inequality and regional priorities.

This last point underscores one final consideration that will be

---

1   Ibid.

examined further in the next chapter: it may be more useful to see security autonomy in a small state as represented on a continuum that includes rather than excludes alignment. The choice is not always between opting for one of the extremes: either remaining completely alone or completely committed inside an alliance. Nor does non-alignment or neutrality necessarily have to mean an absence of international influence. Rather, alignments take on various forms and degrees. A small state may be aligned in some security-related fields but rely purely on its own resources in others. While mediator or active neutrality can be a powerful instrument in the context of a small state's soft or alternative power strategy as we have seen in the case of Switzerland and other small states in recent times.

CHAPTER 5

Small States, Alliances and Security

Alliances are a central concept in international affairs and a principal example of how states work out arrangements to survive in an anarchic international system. Alliances can be bilateral, regional or multilateral in make-up and formal or informal in terms of their entry requirements, rules and regulations and operating procedures.[1] They generally include "mutual expectations of some degree of policy coordination on security issues under certain conditions in the future."[2] Traditionally, alliances have also tended to be written agreements that include a promise by the signatory states to assist each other in a military conflict or at least a commitment to remain neutral in any future conflict. Such agreements can also include a promise to refrain from conflict with third parties and to provide cooperation in order to defuse or prevent conflicts before they begin.[3]

This underscores the fact that the main, though not only, component of traditional security alliances is military and that their primary function is collective defense intended to protect participants from external threats.[4] Alliances tend to have four elements: a strategic objective; a common defense strategy; agreement on how to implement in practice the agreed

---

1 Stephen Walt, *The Origins of Alliances* (Ithaca, NY: Cornell University Press, 1987), 1.
2 M. Barnett and J. Levy, "Domestic Sources of Alliances and Alignments: The Case of Egypt, 1962–1973," *International Organization* 45, no. 3 (1991): 369–395.
3 Brett Leeds, Jeffrey Ritter, Sara Mitchell and Andrew Long, "Alliance Treaty Obligations and Provisions, 1815–1944," *International Interactions* 28, no. 3 (2002): 237–260.
4 John S. Duffield, "Alliances", in *Security Studies: An Introduction*, eds. Paul D. Williams and Matt McDonald (London and New York: Routledge, 2018), 267–281.

defense strategy; and agreement on operational military issues.[1] In terms of categorizing alliances further, one can distinguish between them according to their purpose, notably between those intended to achieve defensive and offensive objectives, and according to their internal structures. Masala, for example, distinguishes between hegemonic alliances in which strong states lead with the consent of smaller powers; imperial alliances in which strong states use coercion to force other members to follow; and egalitarian alliances, in which all members are equal in terms of the decision-making and operational aspects of the alliance.[2]

One can also distinguish alliances in terms of their planned longevity. For example, permanent alliances like NATO are intended to endure over the decades. On its establishment in 1949, NATO's underlying premise was a military alliance based on the principles of collective defense and security. Its members looked to the leadership of a powerful actor at the center—the United States—that was capable of capitalizing on high levels of material power, legitimacy and trust to hold the alliance together despite local divisions and rivalries.[3] On the other hand, ad hoc informal coalitions with an issue-specific focus, like the Saudi-led Yemen war coalition, established in 2015, are only intended to continue for as long as the threat lasts.[4]

The previous chapter underscored that all states face the fundamental security policy choice between autonomy and self-reliance on the one hand and gaining help and support through alliances on the other. It also demonstrated how small states that choose not to align with other countries on security issues normally opt instead for a policy of neutrality. At the

---

1 Chae-Sung Chun, "Theoretical Approaches to Alliance: Implications on the R.O.K.-U.S. Alliance," *Journal of International and Area Studies* 7, no. 2 (December 2000): 71–88.
2 Carlo Masala, "Alliance", in *Routledge Handbook of Security Studies*, eds. Myriam Dunn Cavelty and Victor Mauer (London and New York: Routledge, 2009), 382–392.
3 Robert Haddick, "The Persian Gulf Needs its Own NATO," *Foreign Policy*, May 18, 2012(Accessed February 20, 2020) https://foreignpolicy.com/2012/05/18/the-persian-gulf-needs-its-own-nato.
4 Rory Miller and Sarah Cardaun, "Multinational Security Coalitions and the Limits of Middle Power Activism in the Middle East: The Case of Saudi Arabia," *International Affairs* 96, no. 6 (2020): 1509–1529.

other end of the spectrum from neutrality is a shelter strategy, which assumes that small states not only need alliances but require an even more extensive form of protection from a larger, friendly state, including ties at the political, economic and social levels. Located in-between the two options of neutrality and shelter lie several alignment strategies that differ in terms of alliance choice and the extent of engagement.

Figure 5.1. The Autonomy-Alignment Continuum.

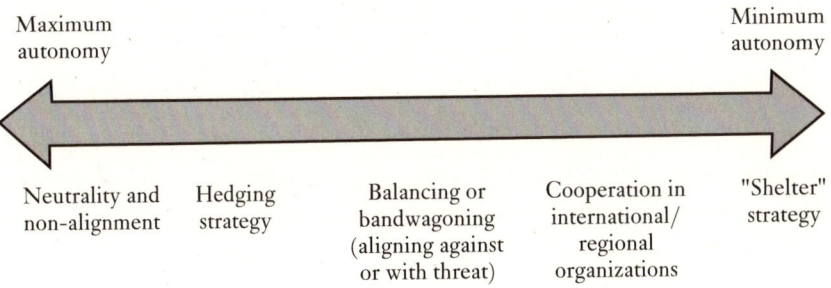

Each type of alignment presented in the above graph entails different potential benefits and costs. On the balance sheet of small state security and survival, in most cases the benefits outweigh the costs. This explains why alliances, though important for all kinds of states, are relatively more important for small states that depend on them for their security and even their survival.

At the same time, on the conceptual level different views exist on why alliances are formed in the first place and why states—small states in particular—join alliances. The traditional assumption of Realist scholars is that states form and participate in alliances out of self-interest and rational motivations in response to common external security threats. In these terms, alliances will appeal to states as a way of maintaining a balance of power as long as those threats continue to exist. This balance of power theory has been propounded over the decades by leading International Relations thinkers including Hans Morgenthau, Hedley Bull, and Kenneth Waltz. It assumes that states aggregate their capabilities in order to balance out a great power. This concept can be understood to be either adversarial, whereby one balances with a big power in a conflict with another big power; or associational, whereby one joins a big power in negotiations in lieu of conflict.[1]

In these traditional realist terms, balancing is both an explanatory framework for why states join alliances—in response to common external security threats—as well as a specific alignment strategy that enables them to achieve required levels of security. Other well-known thinkers have looked to refine the balance of power theory. In the mid-1980s, to take one notable example, Stephen Walt introduced the balance of threats theory. This argued, amongst other things, that alliance formation and participation can be viewed as self-interested behavior between states who hold a shared belief in the benefits of strategic alignment that exhibits structural balance.[2]

Neo-liberals believe that states are rational self-interested actors that are also pre-disposed to cooperation, and that anarchy does not prevent cooperative interactions to the mutual benefit of all involved. On this basis, alliances serve as forms of international institutions that influence the behavior of member states, regulate their interactions, and ultimately facilitate their cooperation. The balance of power then, from a liberal perspective, is often a process of institution-building. Alignment emphasizes the intrinsic benefits of cooperation and institutions including mutual accountability, a general reduction of uncertainty and increased information about the other allies and the wider security environment. In short, cooperation in liberal terms can itself be a "reward."[3]

The Liberal assumption is that alliances are a response to a more complex conception of security and national interest than that offered by

---

1 Richard Little, *The Balance of Power in International Relations: Metaphors, Myths and Models* (Cambridge: Cambridge University Press, 2007).
2 Brian Healy and Arthur Stein, "The Balance of Power in International History: Theory and Reality," *Journal of Conflict Resolution* 17, no. 1 (1973): 33–61; Stephen M. Walt "Alliance Formation and the Balance of World Power," *International Security* 9, no. 4 (1985): 3–43 and "Testing Theories of Alliance Formation: The Case of Southwest Asia," *International Organization* 42, no. 2 (1988): 275–316; Walter W. Powell and Paul J. DiMaggio, *The New Institutionalism in Organizational Analysis* (Chicago: University of Chicago Press, 1991).
3 Masala, "Alliances"; Celeste A. Wallander, "Institutional Assets and Adaptability: NATO After the Cold War," *International Organization* 54, no. 4 (Autumn 2000): 705–735.

Realism. Most importantly, cooperation goes beyond physical security and exhibits rules and practices that constrain governments from all-out war. This is often done by the establishment of norms, sometimes as a process of policy emulation intended to solve particular problems, and sometimes as a way of gaining legitimacy by mimicking external models, a process referred to as mimetic adoption in the literature.

From this perspective, regional organizations (ROs) are important forms of security alliances, especially when they develop into long-lasting cooperative endeavors on matters encroaching on sovereignty. As ROs evolve and mature, their status as legitimate entities in the international system increase and they become, what Maoz has termed, "effective modifiers of self-centered national behavior" and promoters of "collective problem solving."[1] Though many ROs are not security alliances in the traditional sense and only a small number including the European Union (EU), and the African Union (AU), use force to restore peace, they are still important alliance options for small states intent on maximizing their security and influence in the system.

From a constructivist perspective, whereby ideas rather than material forces define relations, the formation, behavior and duration of alliances are not to be explained in terms of capabilities, threats or the state's natural predisposition toward cooperation in international affairs. Instead, alliances are the outcome of shared identity, values and norms between states with similar internal political and cultural makeups.[2] Adler and Greve have argued that regions can be "socially constructed ... collective entities as well as merely territorial ones."[3]

When combined with Hurrell's argument that one should not draw an overly sharp distinction between power-based and identity-based accounts of regions, it is possible to view multilateral frameworks whose members are bound by identity and spread out over different continents

---

1 Zeev Maoz, "Domestic Politics of Regional Security: Theoretical Perspectives and Middle East Patterns," *Journal of Strategic Studies* 26, no. 3, (2003): 9–48.
2 John S. Duffield, "Alliances," 273.
3 Emanuel Adler and Patricia Greve, "When Security Community Meets Balance of Power: Overlapping Regional Mechanism of Security Governance," *Review of International Studies* 35, no. 1 (2009): 59–84.

as forms of security alliances and organizations. One example is the long-existing "Five Eyes" intelligence alliance.[1] Founded in 1946 under the multilateral UK/USA Agreement for Joint Intelligence, and comprising the United Kingdom, the United States, Australia, Canada and New Zealand, its continued existence over the last eight decades has arguably been as much a function of shared anglosphere identity and the cultural affinity of member states as a response to shared security concerns and strategic interests.[2]

Explaining Alliance Formation and Duration

One can understand the formation and duration of alliances by distinguishing between system-level explanations and state-level explanations. Most realist approaches are system-level, but not all system level macro-theories are realist. Many other factors can play a role in alliance formation and in a small states' motives for joining alliances, including the particular characteristics of the region in question as well as those that define the wider international system. The existence of other alliances, international or regional organizations will also influence alignment decisions. This raises the important question of whether or not foreign policy choices always reflect the state or its security interests. Sometimes foreign policy choices such as alignment decisions may reflect the fact that the state is under severe pressure or in a situation in which it is forced to take spontaneous decisions without the time or opportunity to consider the potential (negative) consequences of such actions.

System-level explanations of alliance formation tend to see states as unitary actors and pay more attention to the system rather than the states' own specific actions or choices. The most famous of these system-level explanations is the classical balance of power theory discussed above. From a systemic perspective, the most important factor is whether the system (international and/or regional) is unipolar, bipolar or multipolar

---

[1] Corey Pfluke, "A History of the Five Eyes Alliance: Possibility for Reform and Additions," *Comparative Strategy* 38, no. 4 (2019): 302–315.

[2] Anthony R. Wells, *Between Five Eyes: 50 Years of Intelligence Sharing* (Oxford: Casemate Publishers, 2020).

in nature. For example, the foreign policy objectives of the system's preeminent powers will all influence the alignment strategies of small states. In particular, whether dominant actors conduct a status-quo or a revisionist foreign policy or act in a benign or threatening way toward small states, will have an important impact. Other systemic factors that will influence alliance decisions include the level of regional engagement of dominant actors in the system, notably the global hegemon if one exists; and the number of active and engaged local and emerging powers operating in the region.[1]

It is also the case that states exist and function on multiple levels in a globalized world across many distinct, if overlapping, systems. The extent to which states are engaged in different systems of relationships or may be involved on multiple levels, will also influence alliance decisions. For example, a state may interact with a global hegemon in a global system and also with a regional hegemon in a regional system. One implication of this is that a security strategy that might appear to be unappealing and costly on one level is actually both attractive and affordable to a small state on another level. Similarly, new institutional arrangements in one system are often a response to wider changes occurring in another part of the system or in the system as a whole—such as the beginning of the Cold War in the late 1940s or the launch of the Global War on Terror (GWOT) in the early 2000s.

State-level explanations of alliance formation and duration do not consider states as unitary actors. Instead, they consider various domestic factors that influence a state to seek alignment in ways that transcend the balance of power and external threats.[2] David's conceptualization of omni-balancing as a way to explain the alignment of developing countries in terms of the threat posed to the regime rather than the state is a useful framework for examining such domestic drivers of alliance formation and

---

[1] Steven Lobell, Neal Jesse and K. Williams, "Why Do Secondary States Choose to Support, Follow or Challenge?," *International Politics* 52, no. 2 (2015): 146–162.

[2] Barnett and Levy, "Domestic Sources of Alliances and Alignments: The case of Egypt, 1962–1973."

endurance.¹ So is the revisionist security approach presented in the work of Maoz, whereby regimes are attracted to alliances not to guard against outside threats but to protect their power from domestic opponents.² From this perspective, small state participation in the informal alliances launched in the Middle East in recent years, like the Yemen War Coalition and the anti-Qatar coalition, can be viewed in some cases as a function of domestic legitimacy and power consolidation through the receipt of aid, diplomatic and military support.

No less relevant is Schweller's work on the balance of interest. This theory goes beyond the traditional understanding of alliances as simply responses to threats (external or internal). It rejects the assumption that states align purely to enhance security. Instead, it argues that states can and will join alliances even if they are not threatened for opportunistic reasons and due to a desire for gains.³ On matters of security, it is also possible that collective action will take place without full policy convergence and where there is an explicitly unequal power relationship between the alliance leader and the subordinate actor as long as membership appears to offer attractive benefits to the latter.⁴ Thinking along these lines is also useful in helping us to understand why various small state actors choose to embrace collective action in the absence of a shared hierarchy of threats.

As noted in the previous chapter, a classic policy of neutrality is one in which the state in question chooses to manage all security affairs without the help of allies. This was the case for European states like Austria, Finland, Sweden, and Switzerland during the Cold War. These were armed neutral states who functioned under the legal definition of neutrality

---

1   Steven R. David, "Explaining Third World Alignment," *World Politics* 43, no. 2 (1991): 233–56.
2   Maoz, "Domestic Politics of Regional Security: Theoretical Perspectives and Middle East Patterns."
3   Randall L. Schweller, "Bandwagoning for Profit: Bringing the Revisionist State Back In," *International Security* 19, no. 1 (1994): 72–107.
4   Chris Clough, "Quid Pro Quo: The Challenges of International Strategic Intelligence Cooperation," *International Journal of Intelligence and CounterIntelligence* 17, no. 4 (2004): 601–13.

as codified in the 1907 Hague Convention. Beyond opting out of security alliances, the choice of neutrality also implies that the neutral state acknowledges that greater security cannot be guaranteed by joining a defense alliance or a collective security organization.[1]

One important benefit of neutrality is that by avoiding involvement in international conflicts, the neutral state avoids entrapment in the conflicts of partners and allies. This alone infers that when neutrality is employed by a small state that is geopolitically irrelevant, it can substantially reduce its risk of being attacked or of becoming involved in conflict. Ireland's policy of neutrality during the Second World War, for instance, enabled it to successfully weather the global conflict without it having to align against either side, thus reducing the likelihood of invasion by either the Allied or Axis powers.

On the other hand, one disadvantage of neutrality is that its usefulness and value changes greatly depending on the evolving nature of the country's strategic relationships. After the Cold War, many if not most of the previously neutral European states abandoned strict neutrality because it was no longer viewed to be the most sensible security strategy. Austria, Finland, Sweden and Ireland all adapted to some extent their traditional defensive postures in favor of cooperative strategies that in some, though not all, cases saw a streamlining of military policy in line with the requirements of the EU and, in certain situations in the post-9/11 era, in line with American requirements also. Switzerland, as noted in the previous chapter, as well as Sweden among this group, embraced a policy of internationalization.

Strict non-alignment or neutrality may be an ineffective or even impossible long-term foreign policy orientation for small states in today's globalized international context and in the security environments that exist across a number of regions. In the post-Cold War era, with the threat of territorial attack greatly diminished, both NATO and the EU adapted and evolved into security and risk management organizations that

---

1   Jean-Marc Rickli, "European Small States' Military Policies After the Cold War: From Territorial to Niche Strategies," *Cambridge Review of International Affairs* 21, no. 3 (September 2008): 307–325.

provided security governance in and for Europe. This made the adoption of a policy favoring autonomy increasingly counterproductive at the same time as the adoption of a cooperative strategy became the most efficient strategic option.[1] As Wivel has summed up in the European context: "Defending autonomy by means of institutional opt-outs has little effect when the greatest threat against state autonomy is the ability of other states to carry out their agenda either inside or outside [EU] institutions."[2]

Alliances: A Cost-Benefit Analysis For Small States

The benefits of alliances in terms of aggregating capabilities and minimizing costs are obvious. Moreover, the small state security dilemma is based around a choice between autonomy (neutrality and or isolation) and influence (alignment and or alliance participation).[3] In other words, alignment or entry into alliances not only tend to increase a small state's security, they also tend to enhance its influence through security cooperation with other states. This is especially true in regions like Europe with a relatively high degree of institutionalized security cooperation.

The European example also holds important lessons for small states in other regions as it creates the circumstances that allow for the "big influence of small allies," as Keohane has put it.[4] This option of convincing larger states to take actions that boost the small state's interests, otherwise known as derivative power, has been addressed in a detail in chapter 1, where it was argued that it is one of the most important instruments for influence available to a small state.[5]

This raises the issue of with whom to align! Traditionally, the two main

---

1 Ibid., 315.
2 Anders Wivel, "The Security Challenge of Small EU Member States: Interests, Identity and the Development of the EU As a Security Actor," *Journal of Common Market Studies* 43, no. 2 (2005): 393–412.
3 Hans Mouritzen, *External Danger and Democracy: Old Nordic Lessons and New European Challenges* (Aldershot: Ashgate, 1997).
4 Robert O. *Keohane*, "The Big Influence of Small Allies," *Foreign Policy* 1, no. 2 (Spring 1997): 161–182.
5 Tom Long, "Small States, Great Power? Gaining Influence Through Intrinsic, Derivative and Collective Power" 185–205.

alternatives have been balancing, which usually entails entering into an alliance against a hegemon with other smaller and medium-sized regional actors who face the same threat. This occurred in the Arab Gulf with the establishment of the GCC in the wake of the Iranian revolution and at the start of the Iran-Iraq war in the early 1980s. Another common option is for the smaller state to bandwagon, which is alignment with the stronger, threatening state. This may be done in order to appease the stronger state or in order to benefit from its strength, for example by sharing in the spoils of victory in the wake of a war.[1]

During the Cold War era these two options were the most important strategic choices, especially for small states. The single most relevant parameter in a country's foreign policy was its posture towards the United States and the Soviet Union. Today, however, things are more complex. Each small state that does not pursue a strict policy of neutrality aligns and cooperates with many different actors, including great powers, emerging powers, middle powers, other small states, as well as international and regional security organizations. Moreover, as mentioned above, states have little choice but to engage in multi-level "games," in which they may pursue balancing on one level and bandwagoning on another level.

However, some insights from the Cold War's emphasis on polarity are still relevant today. Although presently, enmity between powerful states is not as severe as it was during the prolonged bipolar era, global and regional competition and rivalry remains an important variable that shapes international relations—one just needs to think of the current clashes between the United States and Russia, and the United States and China respectively. At the same time, small states also still need to pay attention to the power constellation at their respective regional levels as the ongoing tensions between India and Pakistan, Israel and Iran, and Saudi Arabia and Iran underscore.

The level of polarity in the modern Middle East has always been exceptionally high and conflictual, and states have always had to position themselves with respect to long-running conflicts, and ideological and

---

1 Stephen Walt, *The Origins of Alliances* (Ithaca, NY: Cornell University Press, 1987).

political divisions. Consequently, alignment choices have always played an even more significant role for small states in the Middle East than in other, more stable and less polarized regions. In these terms, each strategic alignment with a local power may automatically entail alienating a rival and result in profound security implications. For this reason, small states may adopt a hedging strategy on the regional level, by signaling ambiguity in regard to their alignments with stronger powers. As a security strategy, hedging sits in-between conciliation and confrontation. However, as Guzansky notes, "hedging is more than sitting on the fence." It is a "systematic strategy" that is different from "pure opportunism" and, unlike neutrality, requires taking active measures.[1]

Small states also adopt strategies that go beyond bandwagoning, balancing or hedging. Notably, alliance shelter, which was defined above, is a unique form of alliance engagement whereby the smaller state agrees to give up "effective control of its political decision-making in specific areas" in return for security and protection.[2] Shelter may come at a significant cost for the small state which tends to have different and fewer capabilities, but also operates according to a different logic from its larger partner in social and economic terms.

When the independent Armenian Republic was invaded by Turkey in 1920, its leaders turned to the Soviet Union for shelter as the lesser of two evils, a relationship that extended over the entire inter-war period and continued during the Cold War. Since regaining its independence in the post-Soviet era, Armenia has actively sought alternative, or complementary, options to domination by Moscow by joining a wide-range of international organizations and regimes, as well as by entering into various agreements with the EU. Interestingly, the militarization of a long-time territorial dispute between Armenia and Azerbaijan over the contested Nagorno-Karabakh region in 2020 underscored the ongoing tensions between Turkey and Armenia, as well as the key role that Russia continues to play

---

1   Yoel Guzansky, "The Foreign-Policy Tools of Small Powers: Strategic Hedging in the Persian Gulf," *Middle East Policy* 22, no. 1 (Spring 2015): 112–122.
2   Alyson J. K., Bailes, Bradley A. Thayer and Baldur Thorhallsson, "Alliance Theory and Alliance "Shelter: The Complexities of Small State Alliance Behaviour," *Third World Thematics: A TWQ Journal* 1, no. 1 (2016): 9–26.

in the affairs of smaller bordering states.[1]

The northern Caribbean island of Cuba provides another pertinent example. It sought and gained economic and political shelter from the Soviet Union during the Cold War. This provided major security benefits and relative influence in the Soviet bloc. At the same time, Cuba found it difficult to gain access to development aid from western-controlled international institutions and was excluded from a number of regional communities that were dominated by the United States. Most famously, in October 1962, Cuba found itself at the center of the thirteen-day missile crisis between Moscow and Washington that almost resulted in a full-scale superpower nuclear exchange. Following the collapse of the Soviet Union, Cuba attempted to leave behind its shelter status in order to overcome its relative isolation. It increased its engagement with international institutions and built economic and political ties with China, as well as more geographically proximate actors including Venezuela and Canada.

One further question relates to whether small states are considered valuable alliance participants and alignment partners by larger powers and, linked to this, whether they offer practical benefits to the alliances that they join. This is a relevant question because it affects the alliance choices available to the small state. Some argue that alliances do not automatically benefit from a large number of smaller members.[2] Kjell Inge Bjerga and Torunn Laugen Haaland have used the Norwegian Armed Forces' case study to demonstrate that small states tend to lack the freedom of maneuver and the institutional capacity required to realize their own ideas about the use of their military forces inside traditional multilateral security alliances. Furthermore, their contribution of forces to multilateral military operations are unlikely to make a real difference to the outcome of the battle. For the same reason, a small member state is unlikely to

---

1 Suzan Fraser, "What lies behind Turkish support for Azerbaijan," *Associated Press*, October 2, 2020 (Accessed January 20, 2021) https://apnews.com/article/turkey-territorial-disputes-azerbaijan-ankara-armenia-9a95d9690569623adedffe8c16f3588d.

2 Olivier Schmitt, "More Allies, Weaker Missions? How Junior Partners Contribute to Multinational Military Operations," *Contemporary Security Policy* 40, no. 1 (2019): 70–75.

suffer military defeat in a decisive way inside an alliance.[1]

As a consequence, small state doctrines at the strategic level have become detached from the question of operational effectiveness and are instead utilized for the purpose of promoting political, legal and ethical messages to a domestic and international audience.[2] This underscores the point made above that small states tend to have limited economic and military means, and therefore can require security cooperation with other states to achieve most, if not all, of their relevant security objectives. At the same time, when the leaders of small states choose to ally with a major actor it will always create an unequal alliance, and will also provide the smaller party with "little leverage to exert against its stronger ally."[3]

In some cases, small states may still make military contributions during times of war and peace. One of the most notable trends that has characterized the development of the armed forces in many small states since the end of the Cold War is the concentration, professionalization and specialization of military units.[4] This might enable the small state to contribute to any alliance it participates in with specific military resources, such as highly-skilled special forces. While larger powers that possess a full range of capabilities across all military sectors may not be interested in availing of such opportunities, having specific martial prowess in a narrow area can often make a small state a valuable member of an alliance in the eyes of its partners.

Powerful states also look to smaller alliance partners for intangible benefits such as "ideological convergence, international solidarity, [and] strategic advantage."[5] Ideological convergence occurs when the smaller

---

1   R. L. Rothstein, *Alliances and Small Powers* (New York: Columbia University Press, 1968), 122.
2   Kjell Inge Bjerga and Torunn Laugen Haaland, "Development of Military Doctrine: The Particular Case of Small States," *Journal of Strategic Studies* 33, no. 4 (2010): 505–533.
3   Rothstein, *Alliances and Small Powers*, 122.
4   Maria E. Burczynska, "Multinational Cooperation: Building Capabilities in Small Air Forces," *European Security* 28, no. 1 (2019): 85–104; Anthony King, *The Transformation of Europe's Armed Forces. From the Rhine to Afghanistan* (Cambridge: Cambridge University Press, 2011).
5   Wouter P. Veenendaal, "Analyzing the Foreign Policy of Microstates: The

state accepts and adopts the position of the patron on key policy issues, such as the GWOT. International solidarity occurs when patrons look to smaller clients to adapt their foreign policy or voting behavior in line with their own positions. One notable example is the decision of Palau, Nauru, the Marshall Islands and the Federated States of Micronesia, a group of some of the world's smallest micro-states located in the western Pacific Ocean region, to oppose Palestine's bid for observer status at the UN in November 2012 in line with the preference of Washington.

Dominant actors can also look to smaller partners to gain strategic advantage including basing rights, by using the territory of the client state to strengthen their own geostrategic positions. Linked to this, major actors can also seek to gain strategic advantage by cooperating with small states outside of formal alliance structures. In late September 2001, in the immediate aftermath of the 9/11 attacks on the US, the Irish government agreed to provide over-flight, landing and refueling rights to US military aircraft. This decision was significant because it raised the issue of whether facilitation of the transportation of thousands of US troops to Afghanistan, and subsequently Iraq, was equivalent to Irish participation in the US-led GWOT and, as such, breached Ireland's constitutionally enshrined policy of neutrality that prohibited membership of any military alliance or mutual defense pact.[1]

It is also the case that the lesson of NATO as well as the US-led alliance system in Asia is that projecting military power from far away requires the cooperation and consent of local allies.[2] NATO succeeded not only because the United States was able to draw on its legitimacy, influence and material power but because local actors accepted and facilitated its leadership. This is another unassuming but important contribution that small actors on the regional level can make to alliances. Even those states that do not make significant military contributions can augment alliance legitimacy through their membership or support. For example, Operation

---

    Relevance of the International Patron-Client Model," *Foreign Policy Analysis* 13, no.3 (2017): 561–577.

[1] Rory Miller, "From 9/11 to the War in Iraq: Irish Responses to the Global War on Terror," *Irish Studies in International Affairs* 16, (2005): 155–174.

[2] Robert Haddick, "The Persian Gulf Needs its own NATO."

Enduring Freedom, 2001, the US-led military operation in Afghanistan against Al-Qaeda and the Taliban that followed the 9/11 attacks, was one of the largest and most diverse military coalitions in history and included eighty member states, including many small states.

According to the international patron-client model, in return for the benefits that they provide, smaller states (clients) receive financial, political or military support from the dominant (patron) state.[1] Alongside these contributions, small states can also make other valuable financial, political or symbolic contributions to alliances. One sees all of these ideas in play in discussions over the possible future establishment of a Middle East Strategic Alliance (MESA or Arab NATO). This is a recent proposal to bring together Egypt, Jordan and the members of the moribund GCC (Saudi Arabia, the UAE, Kuwait, Qatar, Oman, Bahrain) in a US-led security alliance.

MESA is viewed as a potential mechanism for ensuring that Washington's regional partners shoulder more of the financial and security burden for regional security while advancing their own and American interests in the wider Middle East.[2] In line with such thinking, the prospective mandate of MESA has widened. Initially it was conceived to provide the Arab Gulf states with the military capabilities to counter Iran. Subsequently, during the Trump presidency, Washington increasingly framed the potential alliance in terms of grander objectives: from countering threats to cyber and energy infrastructure to playing a role in conflict resolution in the wider region.[3]

---

1 Veenendaal, "Analyzing the Foreign Policy of Microstates: The Relevance of the International Patron-Client Model."
2 Marwan Kabalan, "Trump's 'Arab NATO' plan to counter Iran is doomed to fail," *Al Jazeera*, August 10, 2018 (Accessed May 20, 2020) https://www.aljazeera.com/indepth/opinion/trump-arab-nato-plan-counter-iran-doomed-fail-180810090115814.html.
3 Yasmine Farouk, "The Middle East Strategic Alliance Has a Long Way To Go," Carnegie Endowment for International Peace, February 8, 2019. https://carnegieendowment.org/2019/02/08/middle-east-strategic-alliance-has-long-way-to-go-pub-78317.

Regional Organizations and Small State Security

Organizational structures, bureaucracies, and institutional frameworks for cooperation in the realm of peace and security differ greatly in terms of sophistication and formality amongst different states, even those in the same region. Nevertheless, more than five decades ago, Rothstein argued that despite these potentially profound differences, the security and survival of small states is best served by the establishment of a community composed of all regional actors big and small.[1]

The US National Security Strategy of May 2010 acknowledged that ROs can be "particularly effective at mobilizing and legitimating cooperation" on a whole range of challenges and problems.[2] In these terms, the engagement of small states in ROs, is another important example of how smaller actors attempt to counterbalance size-related difficulties by finding effective ways to cope with and manage challenging external environments and a variety of exogenous shocks. This is especially the case if the institution in question, in this case the RO, offers small states security options not previously or currently available elsewhere.[3]

Of course, the extent that the RO is capable of meeting the security needs of the small state member will depend on a number of factors including the RO's legitimacy; the mutual obligation between members; sufficient institutional capabilities and operational capacity; and the presence of a motivated group of core actors who can shape perceptions and lead the RO in any agreed joint action.[4]

---

1   Rothstein, *Alliances and Small Powers*, 34–6.
2   This document noted, in particular, the role of NATO, the Organization for Security Cooperation in Europe (OSCE), the Organization of the Islamic Conference (OIC), the African Union, as well as ASEAN, the EU and the GCC. See US National security strategy, May 1, 2010. https://obamawhitehouse.archives.gov/sites/default/files/rss_viewer/national_security_strategy.pdf.
3   Alyson J.K. Bailes and Baldur Thorhallsson, "Instrumentalizing the European Union in Small State Strategies," *Journal of European Integration* 35, no. 2 (2013): 99–115.
4   See Christopher Hill, "The Capability-Expectations Gap, or Conceptualizing Europe's International Role," *Journal of Common Market Studies* 31, no. 3 (September 1993): 305–328; Charlotte Bretherton and John Volger, *The European Union as a Global Actor* (London and New York: Routledge, 1999);

As noted above, ROs that fulfil these criteria offer opportunities for small states to respond successfully to external vulnerabilities by promoting and protecting their security and defense interests on the regional level. For example, since the end of the Cold War, EU membership has provided the small Baltic states of Estonia, Latvia and Lithuania, an opportunity, alongside their NATO membership, to engage the West as a way of negotiating with the East.[1] The Estonian case is particularly interesting because it embraced the soft security benefits offered by the EU and was willing, in return, to accept some costs of membership. At the same time, Estonia also prioritized a strong attachment to NATO.[2] This underscores the point that while the need for security can be a driver for entry into ROs, it can also influence the extent and form of a small state's engagement once inside.

Entry into any multilateral institution will have an impact on all states that join regardless of their size. For small states, in particular, membership of ROs can modify national strategic agendas and discourses.[3] It has been widely argued, for example, that as in the case of traditional security alliances, small states have little choice but to accept the authority of large states inside ROs, because size is as an important factor in determining a state's influence in all forms of cooperative institutions.[4]

On this basis, it is also argued that the dominant actors in the RO, known in the literature as "activity leaders," play the most significant roles

---

Stephen Kingah and Luk Van Langenhove,"Determinants of a Regional Organisation's Role in Peace and Security: The African Union and the European Union Compared," *South African Journal of International Affairs* 19, no. 2, (2012): 201–222.

[1] Jeremy W. Lamoreaux and David J. Galbreath, "The Baltic States As 'Small States': Negotiating The 'East' By Engaging The 'West'," *Journal of Baltic Studies* 39, no. 1 (2008): 1–14.

[2] E. Männik, "EU and the Aspirations of Applicant Small States: Estonia and the Evolving CESDP," *Current Politics and Economics of Europe* 11, no. 1 (2002): 77–90.

[3] Bailes and Thorhallsson, "Instrumentalizing the European Union in Small State Strategies."

[4] Diana Panke, *Small States in the European Union: Coping with Structural Disadvantages* (Farnham: Ashgate, 2010).

in the key policy areas of defense and security. At the same time, the foreign policy autonomy of small states can also often increase or decline following entry into an RO.[1] Throughout the Cold War, Austria had an active and high-profile foreign policy program based around its neutrality, a commitment to international law, and outspoken advocacy on key international issues including the Arab-Israeli conflict. After its entry into the EU in 1995, the country's role as a "natural born peacemaker on the global stage" diminished greatly.[2] Denmark's entry into the EU in 1973 had the opposite effect. EU membership contributed to the transformation of the country from an anti-militaristic and multilateral member of the Nordic bloc into an activist foreign policy actor and participant in military endeavors including the American invasion of Iraq in 2003.[3]

In both of these cases, specific domestic factors played a role alongside the influence of RO membership in determining the level of Austrian and Danish activism inside the EU. Nevertheless, as Thorhallsson has argued, size is a significant factor in determining the behavior of the smaller states in the decision-making process of ROs. Due to a lack of surplus resources, small member states tend to prioritize their efforts on the most important policy areas and also use different instruments than larger member states in order to achieve their goals.[4] In line with this, small states inside ROs face disadvantages in shaping policies due to their weak bargaining power, and limited financial and human resources.

---

1 G.P. Sharp, "Small State Foreign Policy and International Regimes: The Case of Ireland and the European Monetary System and the Common Fisheries Policy," *Millennium: Journal of International Studies* 16, no. 1 (1987): 55–72.

2 Carmen Gebhard, "Is Small Still Beautiful? The Case of Austria," *Swiss Political Science Review* 19, no. 3 (2013): 279–297.

3 P. Hansen, "Adaptive Behavior of Small States: The Case of Denmark and the European Community," in *Sage International Yearbook of Foreign Policy Studies*, ed. J. McGowan (London: Sage, 1974), 143–174; Anders Wivel, "From Peacemaker to Warmonger? Explaining Denmark's Great Power Politics," *Swiss Political Science Review* 19, no. 3 (2013): 298–321; Rasmus Brun Pedersen, "Danish Foreign Policy Activism: Differences in Kind or Degree?," *Cooperation and Conflict* 47, no. 3 (2012): 331–349.

4 B. Thorhallsson, *The Role of Small States in the European Union* (Burlington, VT: Ashgate, 2000).

That said, as Nasra has argued, even small states with limited resources may not be small in terms of their influence inside the RO.[1] El Mallakh drew on the early years of the GCC to make the case that integration into the local RO can directly increase the status and influence as well as the security of small states with an outward-looking perspective.[2] This is one reason why small states are attracted to ROs, because the multiplier effect is bigger for them than their larger counterparts inside the same institutions. One interesting consequence of such small state policy success inside ROs is that it can signal a decline in their commitment to pursue an independent security policy, especially if doing so constrains or complicates attempts to promote their security priorities within the RO.[3]

In her work, Panke has demonstrated the effectiveness of small states inside ROs when they are able to apply a variety of strategies to counterbalance size-related difficulties. Specifically, they can become important policy shapers inside the RO if they are selective in focusing on key policy areas. This is especially true if they focus on normative issues and are able to harness their resources inside the institution's decision-making mechanisms by engaging in agenda-setting or chairing meetings.[4] Grøn and Wivel have designated this pro-active small state behavior inside the RO as a function of lobbying, self-interested mediation, and norm entrepreneurship.[5] Mobilizing such "compensatory power" is much

---

1   Skander Nasra, "Governance in EU Foreign Policy: Exploring Small State Influence," *Journal of European Public Policy* 18, no. 2 (2011): 164–180.
2   Bjorn G. Olafsson, *Small States in the Global System: Analysis and Illustrations from the Case of Iceland* (VT: Ashgate, 1988), 154.
3   Sharp, "Small State Foreign Policy and International Regimes: The Case of Ireland and the European Monetary System and the Common Fisheries Policy"; B. Thorhallsson, "Consequences of a Small Administration: The Case of Iceland," *Current Politics and Economics of Europe* 11, no. 1 (2002): 61–76.
4   Diana Panke, "Small states in the European Union: Structural Disadvantages in EU Policymaking and Counter-Strategies," *Journal of European Public Policy* 17, no. 6 (September 2010): 799–817; Diana Panke, "Small States in Multilateral Negotiations. What have we learned?," *Cambridge Review of International Affairs* 25, no. 3, (September 2012): 387–398.
5   Caroline Howard Grøn and Anders Wivel, "Maximizing Influence in the European Union after the Lisbon Treaty: From Small State Policy to Smart

more possible inside ROs that have independent institutions that can stand up to pressure from major member states, and which respond well to the technocratic endeavors of smaller members.

Sweden's success in driving forward the adoption of the EU Programme for the Prevention of Violent Conflict is one notable example of a small state using available instruments to achieve influence over an RO's security policies.[1] Finally, Jakobsen has challenged the view that the development of the EU's European Security and Defence Policy (ESDP) was dominated by the three major member states—the United Kingdom, France and Germany. Instead, he has argued that the small Nordic countries had a significant, and at times even decisive, influence on ESDP. Notably, they put civilian crisis management on the ESDP agenda and successfully kept it there in the face of strong opposition from France; they also played important roles with respect to proposing and designing its concepts and institutions; and they have consistently made disproportionate mission contributions in terms of both personnel and financial resources.[2]

State Strategy," *Journal of European Integration* 33, no. 5 (2011): 523–539.

1 Annika Björkdahl, "Norm Advocacy: A Small State Strategy to Influence the EU," *Journal of European Public Policy* 15, no. 1 (2008): 135–154.

2 Peter Viggo Jakobsen, "Small States, Big Influence: The Overlooked Nordic Influence on the Civilian ESDP," *Journal of Common Market Studies* 47, no. 1 (2009): 81–102.

CHAPTER 6

The Blockade of Qatar: Small States, Foreign Policy and Security Options

The renowned Kuwaiti scholar Hassan Ali Al-Ebraheem once counselled his fellow citizens of the Arab Gulf to remember that they live in a dangerous neighborhood.[1] Following its launch in June 2017 until it was abandoned in January 2021, the blockade of Qatar by some of its closest economic and security partners inside the GCC served as a stark reminder of how dangerous and unpredictable the region can be. It also provided a constant reminder of the vulnerabilities that small states face in protecting their security, which we defined in an earlier chapter as the "alleviation of threats to cherished values."[2]

From the perspective of small state security studies, the blockade of Qatar is an excellent example of a crisis in which a larger opponent with expansionist or revisionist goals uses hybrid warfare to target a smaller state to achieve its strategic objectives. From the outset, the intention of the blockading countries was to destabilize Qatar and pressure decision-makers in Doha to accede to their demands. The overt and covert methods adopted by the Saudi-UAE led anti-Qatar coalition in pursuit of their goals included disinformation, cyber-attacks, economic pressure and diplomatic isolation at a level that, in the words of the NATO definition of hybrid warfare, remained "below the threshold of formally declared warfare."[3]

---

1 See Hassan Ali Al-Ebraheem, *Kuwait and the Gulf: Small States and the International System*, 2nd ed. (London: Routledge, 2016).
2 Paul D. Williams and Matt McDonald, "An Introduction to Security Studies," in *Security Studies: An Introduction*, eds. P. D. Williams and M. McDonald (London/New York: Routledge, 2018), 1–13.
3 "NATO's Response to Hybrid Threats," August 8, 2019. https://www.nato.int/cps/en/natohq/topics_156338.htm.

In Doha, initial concerns not only revolved around the long-term implications of this attack on economic and political sovereignty but, more immediately, the availability of fresh food, the sudden drop in the value of the stock market and worries over the ambitious plans for the upcoming FIFA World Cup in 2022. There were also real concerns that the coalition ranged against Qatar might follow up its strategy of isolation with military action, alongside a sustained campaign of cyber and economic warfare intended to paralyze the Qatari economy or even force regime change.

The blockade was not militarized in the conventional sense in its first phase or subsequently, and after overcoming the initial psychological and financial shock, daily life in Qatar returned to normal for most. Indeed, the blockade even presented opportunities for Qatar to demonstrate its rising independence across a number of key sectors. For example, within months of the blockade's start Qatar had achieved, in the words of Tareq Al-Ansari, "a multi-scale and multi-dimensional transformation" in the country's self-sufficiency in the dairy sector, which in turn contributed significantly to Qatar's long-term food security strategies.[1] By early 2018, Qatar's Amir, H.H. Sheikh Tamim bin Hamad Al-Thani was able to refer confidently to the "failed blockade" before an influential audience at the Munich Security Conference. Interestingly, in the same speech, Qatar's leader noted how the events of the previous six months had demonstrated "how small states can use diplomacy and strategic economic planning to weather the storms of aggression from larger, ambitious neighbors."[2]

As previous chapters have demonstrated, there does not exist any agreement in the literature on what constitutes a small state due to differences in culture, geography, history, natural resources, and levels of development. Moreover, no two small states share the same vulnerabilities or challenges, something that serves to further differentiate them from one

---

[1] Tareq Al-Ansari, "Food Security: The Case of Qatar," in *The Gulf Crisis: The View from Qatar*, ed. Rory Miller (Doha: Hamad bin Khalifa University Press, 2018), 28–38.

[2] "Speech of Qatar Emir at Munich Security Conference," *The Peninsula*, February 16, 2018 (Accessed June 20, 2020) https://thepeninsulaqatar.com/article/16/02/2018/Speech-of-Qatar-Emir-at-Munich-Security-Conference.

another. Nevertheless, if the assessment made by Qatar's Amir at Munich is correct then the country's handling of the blockade demonstrates that small states can use asymmetric sources of power in order to absorb external shocks, deter hostile opponents, and achieve defensive and offensive strategic objectives even at times of severe crisis. It also undermines the conventional wisdom set out in the theoretical literature and discussed extensively in the earlier chapters of this book that sovereign states who can claim an advantage over their adversaries in terms of the traditional measures of power—size of population and territory, military capabilities and GNP—will inevitably emerge as victors from any military, diplomatic or economic clash.

Qatar: From Weak Micro-State to Strong Small State

For much of the time after Qatar gained independence and joined the United Nations (UN) in 1971, it was classified as a micro-state on the basis of the size of its population and territory.[1] In its first two decades after independence, in typical small state fashion, it was also preoccupied with domestic economic development rather than foreign policy issues.[2] After H.H. Sheikh Hamad bin Khalifa Al-Thani came to power in 1995, Qatar's growing population, rapid domestic development, ambitious program of state-branding, and rising status as a global gas power resulted in its transition from a micro-state to a small, developing, state of some standing.

In line with its evolving status, from the late 1990s until the Arab Spring of 2011, Qatar developed into a significant foreign policy actor in the Arab regional system. The first pillar of this ambitious program included international engagement, financial diplomacy and conflict mediation and resolution. To give one example, in mid-November 2001, shortly after Al-Qaeda's attacks on New York and Washington D.C., Qatar hosted delegations from 142 countries at the WTO ministerial meeting. This

---

1 For a detailed discussion of microstates see G.L. Reid, *The Impact of Very Small Size on the International Relations Behavior of Microstates* (London: Sage, 1974).
2 Robert Good, "State-Building as Determinant of Foreign Policy in the New States," in *Neutralism and Non-Alignment: The New States in World Affairs*, ed. L. Martin (New York: Praeger, 1962), 3–12.

summit ran smoothly without any incident at a time of high alert across the international community. Its success provided Qatar with massive global exposure. The subsequent rounds of trade negotiations that followed the meeting, dubbed the Doha Round, continued to shine a positive spotlight on the kingdom.

The second pillar of its program revolved around a flourishing security relationship with the United States which, as Wright has noted, provided Qatar with "a greater degree of autonomy in foreign policy."[1] Following the 9/11 attacks of September 2001, Qatar also took advantage of its status as home to a major US airbase, as well as one of the largest overseas American military pre-positioning bases, to capitalize on the unprecedented strains in the US-Saudi relationship. Notably, in the last few months of 2002, hundreds of staff, about one quarter of Central Command's (CENTCOM) entire operational command, moved from their headquarters in Tampa, Florida, to Qatar to participate in military exercises.

This was the first forward deployment of Central Command staff since preparation for the war in Kuwait began in 1990. The practical implications of this move were widely understood. It appeared that Qatar was increasingly becoming Washington's preferred location for its command and control headquarters in any war in Iraq. In early 2003, in the run-up to the launch of the invasion of Iraq, an estimated six thousand CENTCOM and other US staff officers, as well as a hundred and twenty fighter planes relocated to various bases on the outskirts of Doha. In April 2003, exactly one month after the American campaign in Iraq began, the Bush administration announced that it was relocating its regional air operations center from Prince Sultan Air Base near Riyadh in Saudi Arabia to the al-Udeid Air base in Qatar.

In the decade and a half since the American invasion of Iraq, Qatar has consolidated its status as the key hub in CENTCOM's warfighting capability. In 2019, for example CENTCOM's deputy commander Major General

---

1 S. Wright, "Foreign Policies with International Reach: The Case of Qatar," in *The Transformation of the Gulf: Politics, Economics and the Global Order*, eds. David Held and Kristian Coates Ulrichsen (London: Routledge 2011).

Chance Saltzman described Qatar as "an exceptional partner."[1] In strategic terms, this achievement can be viewed as the culmination of Qatar's efforts to use the full range of instruments of power at its disposal to achieve its strategic goals by aligning itself with Washington's defense agenda.

By the mid-2000s, Qatar's external activism was also facilitated by the unprecedented influence of Al-Jazeera, Qatar's cable news network, founded in 1996 by the new Amir, one year after he rose to power. As it grew in popularity, this network developed into a major irritant of policymakers from North Africa to the Levant. Within five years of its launch, almost every Arab government had lodged a formal complaint with the Qatari government over the network's critical reporting.[2]

Another driver of Qatar's evolving relevance as a small state in the international system was its rising status as a major player in the global gas markets. During the 1990s, oil accounted for more than one third of Qatar's annual GDP. To put this into perspective, the financial, property, industrial and manufacturing sectors combined only accounted for around one fifth of GDP. The decision to use existing and future oil revenues to build up the country's underdeveloped gas sector was both very costly and very risky as it is much more expensive to extract gas than drill for oil.

This was particularly true in the Qatari case because much of its gas was located in the deep waters off its northern coast, in particular the North Field, the largest natural gas field in the world. Another obstacle at this time was the lack of existing pipelines needed to ship gas to some key target markets like India. Other potential markets in Asia, notably Japan and South Korea, had existing pipeline access but were already buying gas from major producers such as Indonesia and Malaysia. Europe, one of the most lucrative markets, already had sufficient pipelines pumping gas from Algeria, Russia and the North Sea.

---

1   "CENTCOM: Pentagon Says No Plans To Move US Military Base Outside Qatar," *The New Arab*, 1 October 2019 (Accessed June 25, 2020) https://english.alaraby.co.uk/news/centcom-there-no-plan-move-qatar-base.

2   Rory Miller and Harry Verhoeven, "Overcoming Smallness: The UAE, Qatar and Strategic Realignment in the Gulf," *International Politics* 57, no. 1 (February 2020): 1–20.

The low oil price during the 1990s also meant that Qatar had less available surplus revenues to spend on the huge setting up costs associated with gas projects. Extracting gas was only one major expense. It also cost billions of dollars to dredge a port in the shallow coastal waters of the Gulf that was fit for purpose, and to build suitable port facilities and infrastructure at Ras Laffan, which by the late 1990s would be transformed into one of the largest gas exporting hubs in the world. Due to a lack of readily available pipelines, Qatar also had to purchase a very expensive fleet of state-of-the-art specialist tankers fitted to transport their gas to customers. The risks attached to this investment were especially high as a number of the key potential buyers of Qatari gas did not have the technology in place at this time to handle such sophisticated gas tankers. Qatar's rapidly developing gas sector not only underscored the country's willingness to take risks. It also underscored its ambitions to become a global as well as regional economic force. By 2004, it was the fastest growing economy in the Middle East. This was fueled by rising oil prices and the diversification of the energy sector away from oil and toward natural gas. It was also driven by massive government investment in the tourism, educational and hospitality sectors that resulted in a boom in construction and real estate development.

In 2004, foreign direct investment into Qatar reached record levels, increasing by more than 1500 percent over the previous year.[1] In that same year, Qatar announced its intention to invest US$25 billion over the next six years to quadruple its gas export capacity in order to become the first country to sell gas to Europe, Asia and North America at the same time. This was on top of the estimated US$70 billion in foreign investment that the kingdom's gas industry would absorb by the mid-2000s. Soon after, Qatar announced its intention to become the world's number one exporter of Liquefied Natural Gas (LNG) by 2011. In December 2010, the same month it was awarded the 2022 FIFA World Cup, and one year ahead of its target date, Qatar's high-risk, high-cost, strategy paid off when it became the world's top exporter of LNG. The revenues that followed Qatar's rising status as a leading player in the global energy market

---

1   *Gulf News*, 20 February 2005.

provided it with the resources for it to continue financing its role as major regional foreign policy actor.

Qatar's foreign policy dynamism in the first decade of the twenty-first century challenges the view in the literature that large states initiate more foreign policy events alone, while small states initiate more joint behavior.[1] It also challenges the view put forward by Handel and others that small states cannot develop an independent policy in international affairs.[2] Perhaps most relevant to the blockade has been Qatar's willingness to compete with, and stand up to, larger foreign policy actors on key regional issues despite differences in size. In part, this was possible due to Qatar's astute engagement in "riyal politic"[3] as one commentator described its innovative use of financial diplomacy in these years.

The channeling of some of the country's significant surplus energy revenues into regional affairs illuminated a willingness to promote an independent foreign policy approach that challenged the interests of much larger actors including Saudi Arabia and Egypt to an extent that no other small state in the Arab world had previously managed. This evolving dynamic became very evident throughout the Arab Spring.

From the earliest days of protest in Tunisia, Al-Jazeera led the way in reporting events on the ground on a minute by minute basis twenty-four hours a day. The network's coverage of the uprising in Tunisia also fueled the initial protests against the Mubarak government in Egypt. Thereafter, the channel played an important role in sustaining the anti-regime sentiment that led to Mubarak's downfall. In Libya, Colonel Gaddafi accused the network of inciting rebels; while a photograph of a slogan on

---

1   M. East, "Size and Foreign Policy Behavior: A Test of Two Models," *World Politics* 25, no.4 (1973): 556–576.
2   Michael Handel, *Weak States in the International System*, 2nd ed. (London: Frank Cass, 1990).
3   Abdullah Baabood, "Dynamics and Determinants of the GCC States' Foreign Policy, with Special Reference to the EU," in *Analyzing Middle East Foreign Policies and the Relationship with Europe*, ed. Gerd Nonneman (London: Routledge, 2005), 145–173.

a wall in the city of Tobruk that read "Freedom=Al Jazeera" went viral and gained worldwide exposure.[1]

On the diplomatic front, Qatar was a major backer of the post-Mubarak Morsi government in Egypt and one of the first countries to recognize Libya's National Interim Transitional Council. It also assumed the daunting role of holding together the international anti-Gaddafi coalition, hosting negotiations between NATO and senior anti-regime militia leaders, and pressuring and lobbying key members of the international community, most notably China, to back the forces of change in Libya.[2]

In July 2011, Qatar also became the first Gulf country to withdraw its ambassador from Syria and close its embassy in Damascus.[3] Qatar then used its rotating presidency of the Arab League to build an Arab consensus in favor of financial and economic sanctions against the Assad regime. In early 2012, in a widely-reported interview with the American broadcaster CBS' flagship news program, 60 Minutes, Qatar's Amir became the first Arab leader to call for military intervention in Syria in order to "stop the killing."[4] This was a very bold move at a time when most of the international community was only willing to provide political support, commit humanitarian supplies or, at the very most, supply covert military aid to the anti-Assad rebels.

The 2017 Blockade: A Small State Responds to Crisis

Qatar's ambitious and multi-dimensional foreign policy engagement during and after the Arab Spring is reflected in the established literature on the country which acknowledges it as an important contemporary

---

1 Rory Miller, *Desert Kingdoms to Global Powers: The Rise of the Arab Gulf* (New Haven: Yale University Press, 2016), 197.
2 Hugh Eakin, "The Strange Power of Qatar," *New York Review*, October 27, 2011, https://www.nybooks.com/articles/2011/10/27/strange-power-qatar/.
3 Eckhart Woertz, "Qatar and Europe's Neglect of the Gulf Region," *Notes Internacionals CIDOB*, 46 (February 2012). https://www.files.ethz.ch/isn/141961/NOTES%2046_WOERTZ_ENG.pdf.
4 "Syria Rejects Qatar Call for Arab Military Intervention," *BBC News*, January 17, 2012 (Accessed June 20, 2020) http://www.bbc.com/news/world-middle-east-16597015.

actor in the Arab regional system.¹ There is also a growing body of work published on Qatar as a small state actor in international affairs.² Despite acknowledging and analyzing underlying tensions between Qatar on the one hand, and Saudi Arabia, the UAE and Bahrain on the other, this extensive literature completely failed to predict that Qatar would soon be the target of an unprecedented diplomatic and economic attack from these three long-time GCC partners, backed up by Egypt and a group of smaller Arab and Muslim states. Indeed, the launch of the embargo was intended to diminish Qatar's regional standing and influence, and remove it as an obstacle to the wider strategic ambitions of the Saudi-UAE axis. It was also intended to ensure that Qatar, as the smaller actor compared to the UAE and Saudi Arabia, fell into line with the increasingly convergent foreign policy and security priorities of its neighbors.

The disparity in size and resources between Qatar and the four core members of the coalition—Saudi Arabia, the UAE, Egypt and Bahrain—is significant. At the time that the embargo was launched they had a combined population that was fifty-five times bigger than Qatar's (137 million compared to 2.5 million); they controlled a combined territory two hundred and seventy nine times larger than the State of Qatar (3,234 million km² compared with 11,521 km²); their combined military spending,

---

1 J. Abadi, "Qatar's Foreign Policy: The Quest for National Security and Territorial Integrity," *Journal of South Asian and Middle Eastern Studies* 27, (2004): 14–37; Lina Khatib "Qatar's Foreign Policy: The Limits of Pragmatism," *International Affairs* 89, no. 2 (2013): 417–432; D. B. Roberts, "Understanding Qatar's Foreign Policy Objectives," *Mediterranean Politics* 17, no. 2 (2012): 233–239.

2 A. F. Cooper and B. Momani, "Qatar and Expanded Contours of Small State Diplomacy," *The International Spectator: Italian Journal of International Affairs* 46, no. 3 (2011): 113–128; Kristian Coates Ulrichsen, "Small States With a Big Role: Qatar and the United Arab Emirates in the Wake of the Arab Spring," *Durham: HH Sheikh Nasser al-Mohammad al-Sabah Publication Series* 3 (2012); Rory Miller and Khalid Al-Mansouri, "Qatar's Foreign Policy Engagement with the European Union: Evolving Priorities of a Small State in the Contemporary Era," *Comillas Journal of International Relations* 5, (2016): 46–64; Mehran Kamrava, *Qatar: Small State, Big Politics* (Ithaca & London: Cornell University Press, 2013); David B. Roberts, *Qatar: Securing the Global Ambitions of a City-State* (London: Hurst, 2017).

based on 2015 figures, was sixteen times greater than Qatar's (US$112,871 billion compared to US$7 billion); while their combined GNP, also based on 2015 figures, was eleven times greater (US$3.49 trillion compared to US$309 billion).

With the start of the crisis, Qatar was transformed overnight from a pro-active international actor into a besieged small state in a hostile regional environment with little choice but to defend its core interests from the much stronger coalition ranged against it. Yet despite the notable power imbalance, for the duration of the blockade Qatar managed to contain successfully its negative impact, and to maintain its political autonomy and economic sovereignty. As previous chapters have noted, states that can achieve economic and political self-reliance will be more difficult for external opponents to divide and rule than ones that are economically dependent on other actors.[1]

As an economic actor, Qatar has always had to deal with exactly the same obstacles that other small states have faced in achieving such self-reliance. It has a small domestic market, high production costs, low economies of scale, and low levels of industrial production. But in recent decades it has also had one massive advantage—the financial resources it has earned from its status as a major global gas exporter. For example, in 2014 and 2015, at a time of falling prices, the country's gas revenues were still US$107 billion and US$60 billion respectively making it the world's wealthiest nation by output per capita.[2]

As argued in chapter 2, small states that embody "creative agency,"[3] in the words of Cooper and Shaw, can achieve a level of strategic flexibility

---

1 S. Kuznets, "Economic Growth of Small Nations," in *Economic Consequences of the Size of Nations*, ed. E. A. G. Robinson (New York: St. Martin's Press, 1960); O. Krantz, "Small European Countries in Economic Internationalisation: An Economic Historical Perspective," Umeå Papers in Economic History, 26, 2006.
2 "Qatar Remains a Leading Player in Oil and Gas," Oxford Business Group, 2016. https://oxfordbusinessgroup.com/overview/market-share-matters-despite-global-price-volatility-country-remains-leading-player-oil-and-gas.
3 Antony F. Cooper and Timothy M. Shaw, "The Diplomacies of Small States at the Start of the Twenty-first Century: How Vulnerable? How Resilient?," In *The Diplomacies of Small States: Between Vulnerability and Resilience*, eds. A. F. Cooper and T. M. Shaw (Basingstoke: Palgrave MacMillan, 2009), 2.

that allows them to implement policies that bring stability and resilience. Baabood, for example, had argued that Qatar's resilience strategy was crucial to the country's economic capacity to withstand the blockade after June 2017.[1] From the earliest months of the blockade, Qatar demonstrated that it was adept at maximizing the surplus financial resources generated by its gas revenues in order to successfully achieve its strategic objectives. These included the import of vital supplies, the opening up of new trade routes, and continued access to international airspace by ensuring the normal functioning of Qatar Airways.

At the same time, Qatar used its financial resources to fund major deals with important external partners, consolidating bilateral ties in the process. Notably, in 2017 it signed a US$14 billion deal with France for jets, armored vehicles, advanced weapons systems and civilian infrastructure. The following year the country signed a US$5 billion agreement with the United Kingdom to buy twenty-four Typhoon Fighter planes.[2] This is evidence that a small country like Qatar can use its economic and financial power to increase international standing, and forge security alliances with larger states. It also reminds us of the point made in an earlier chapter that a small state can pursue a successful foreign and security policy by using soft power to "enlarge virtually," as Chong has termed it.[3]

Brannagan and Giulianotti's work on Qatari soft power, which was published following the start of the blockade, provides a model of soft power dynamics including counteracting factors that account for the

---

1 Abdullah Baabood, "Qatar's Resilience Strategy and Implications for State-Society Relations," IAI Working Papers 17, Rome: Istituto Affari Internazionali, 2017.

2 Hadeel Al Sayegh, "Qatar Flexes Financial Muscle with 12 billion Euros of French Deals," *Reuters*, December 7, 2017 (Accessed May 20, 2020) https://www.reuters.com/article/us-qatar-france-contracts/qatar-flexes-financial-muscle-with-12-billion-euros-of-french-deals-idUSKBN1E1162; Sylvia Pfeifer, "BAE Ties Up £5bn Qatar Deal for Typhoon Fighters," *Financial Times*, September 18, 2019 (Accessed May 20, 2020) https://www.ft.com/content/b68e59a6-bb4c-11e8-8274-55b72926558f.

3 Alan Chong, "Small State Soft Power Strategies: Virtual Enlargement in the Cases of the Vatican City State and Singapore," *Cambridge Review of International Affairs* 23, no. 3 (2010): 383–405.

negative outcomes of soft power strategies.[1] The authors distinguish three stages that are crucial to the process of soft power acquisition by any small state: (1) the ways in which the state's soft power resources lead to possible power outcomes; (2) the ways in which the conversion of these resources into successful outcomes depend on the (inter)subjectivities of soft power audiences; (3) the impact of soft disempowerment on audience evaluations of foreign and domestic policies.[2]

This third factor describes a situation in which soft power can "backfire," especially in terms of causing reputational damage which otherwise might not occur. It provides one reason why the effectiveness of soft power as an asset in the small state arsenal is still a widely debated, if not hotly contested, matter. It also serves as a reminder that in the final account soft power is still a form of power that is by no means guaranteed to increase the world's love for you. If used correctly, soft power will also impede the interests of others and make you enemies. It can, in other words, create the same objections and hostilities among competitors, and even partners, as other harder, more tangible, instruments of power that are available to sovereign states.

That said, Aaltola, Sipilä and Vuorisalo have argued that "de-territorial agility and innovativeness" can make up for traditional power disparities between weak states and larger and stronger actors in the international system.[3] Early in the crisis, Qatar demonstrated impressive agility and innovation in persuading important external actors in Europe, Africa, Asia, and the wider Arab and Muslim worlds to remain neutral. Qatar was also highly effective in negotiating an upgrade in bilateral security relations with Turkey in order to balance the hard power threat posed by Saudi Arabia and the UAE on its borders. As Qatar's Minister of State for Defense and Deputy Prime Minister, H.E. Dr. Khalid bin Mohamed Al-Attiyah, explained at a meeting in London in January 2018, this is a

---

[1] P. M. Brannagan and R. Giulianotti, "The Soft Power–Soft Disempowerment Nexus: The Case of Qatar," *International Affairs* 94, no. 5 (2018): 1139–1157.
[2] Ibid.
[3] Mika Aaltola, Joonas Sipilä, Valtteri Vuorisalo "Securing Global Commons: A Small State Perspective," The Finnish Institute of International Affairs, Working Paper 71, June 2011.

"strategic partnership to enhance and diversify [Qatar's] defense capabilities."[1]

Over the second half of 2017, Qatar also convinced the US government to reaffirm publicly its security commitment to Qatar after an initial period when the Trump administration appeared to sympathize with the actions of the anti-Qatar coalition. This culminated in the first high-level annual US-Qatari Strategic Dialogue in Washington D.C. in January 2018. During that meeting, US Secretary of State Rex Tillerson referred to Qatari sovereignty and the US commitment to that sovereignty on three separate occasions. The joint statement published after the meeting by the US state department and Qatar's foreign ministry also focused on Qatar's sovereignty and Washington's commitment to "deter and confront" threats to Qatar's territorial integrity. Though this was not a legal obligation, it was explicit American backing for Qatar in the context of the blockade.[2]

To some extent, this Qatari focus on winning over the two biggest military powers in the Middle East—first Turkey and then the US—does give credence to the conventional view in the literature that small states require a powerful protector when challenged by larger neighbors. On the other hand, the success of Qatar in binding both countries to its security underscores how the country, despite its size, has been able to consolidate its position as a diplomatic player of the first rank and to make the case for its strategic value even when isolated and under siege. Speaking in early 2018, then US Secretary of Defense James N. Mattis, a former CENTCOM commander, acknowledged the importance of US military bases in Qatar to CENTCOM's warfighting capabilities. The following March, in written testimony before the Senate Armed Services Committee, then head of CENTCOM, General Joseph L. Votel, expounded on how, over the

---

1 "A Conversation with Qatar Defence Minister H.E. Dr. Khalid bin Mohammad Al-Attiyah," Royal United Services Institute (RUSI), January 17, 2018. https://www.rusi.org/events/members-events/a-conversation-with-qatar-defence-minister-he-dr-khalid-bin-mohammad-al-attiyah.

2 Joint Statement of the Inaugural United States-Qatar Strategic Dialogue, US Department of State, Office of the Spokesman, 20 January 2018 https://www.state.gov/joint-statement-on-the-u-s-qatar-strategic-dialogue/.

previous twenty years, Qatar had provided "invaluable regional access through basing and freedom of movement."[1]

Qatar's success in consistently aligning itself with Washington's regional defense agenda since the late 1990s proved its value for the country following the launch of the blockade. The bases issue highlights how a small state can embrace long-term strategic options that can help overcome structural limitations in times of vulnerability. Though its relationship with the US inevitably increased Qatar's vulnerability to entrapment and abandonment at the hands of a major global power, it also contradicted the claim made by Rothstein that small states tend to ignore long-term planning in order to ensure short-term stability. On some level, this scenario also underscores the importance of Schweller's work on the balance of interest in explaining alignment in the international system, as the Qatari success in binding Turkey to its side as the blockade evolved can be viewed as a good example of a state, in this case Turkey, participating in an alliance even if it is not directly threatened due to a desire for gains.[2]

In all these endeavors, Qatar clearly demonstrated that while military power is vital for national security, the intelligent use of other sources of power can also play an important role in contributing to small state stability in times of crisis. This was particularly true in regard to domestic unity and social cohesion. Campbell and Hall, as noted earlier in this book, have made the case that small, culturally homogeneous countries with a strong national identity have institutional advantages that tend to enhance their long-term socioeconomic performance. In particular, they can coordinate policies in ways that allow for "cooperation, sacrifice, flexible maneuvering, and concerted state action in the national interest."[3]

---

1 Statement of General Joseph l. Votel, Commander US Central Command before the Senate Armed Services Committee on the posture of US Central Command, March 13, 2018 (Accessed February 1, 2021) https://www.armed-services.senate.gov/download/votel_03-13-18.
2 Randall L. Schweller, "Bandwagoning for Profit: Bringing the Revisionist State Back In," *International Security* 19, no. 4 (1994): 72–107.
3 John L. Campbell and John A. Hall, "National Identity and the Political Economy of Small States," *Review of International Political Economy* 16, no.4 (2009), 547–572.

All occurred on the domestic level inside Qatar during the crisis, underscoring the important point made by Papadakis and Starr that state power can emerge from factors other than straightforward material resources.[1]

As the literature has argued, the smaller the state the more it relies on international norms and laws and the role of international organizations in upholding the principles of sanctity for the territorial integrity and independence of even the smallest members of the international system.[2] This has made it a priority of small actors faced with regional threats, like the one Qatar faced at the hands of the Saudi-UAE coalition ranged against it, to attempt to locate and promote confidence building measures and informal mechanisms, in particular assurance mechanisms, that can lead to dialogue and a gradual process of regional reconciliation between the feuding parties. Such a re-imagining of strategic relations is vital to all small states in order to stem the insecurity and instability that is fueled by such crises. This is especially true for Qatar, given its location in a high-stakes region at the center of the international security and financial systems at a time when the main regional institution—the GCC—had proven itself unable to play an effective conflict management role.

In the absence of the GCC option and with bilateral negotiations posing the risk of entrapment, in February 2018, Qatar's Amir, H.H. Sheikh Tamim bin Hamad Al-Thani, used his speech at the Munich Security Conference to propose a "broader platform for dialogue and negotiation," as the country's foreign minister subsequently described it.[3] The first part of this Qatari proposal envisioned a "framework for regional governance,

---

1   M. Papadakis and H. Starr, "Opportunity, Willingness, and Small States: The Relationship Between Environment and Foreign Policy," in *New Directions in the Study of Foreign Policy*, eds. C. F. Hermann, C. W. Kegley, J. Rosenau (Boston: Allen & Unwin, 1987), 409–432.
2   Barry Bartmann, "Meeting the Needs of Microstate Security," *The Round Table: The Commonwealth Journal of International Affairs* 91, no. 365 (2002): 361–374.
3   Mohammed bin Abdulrahman Al-Thani, "End the Blockade of Qatar," *New York Times*, June 5, 2018 (Accessed, March 12, 2021) https://www.nytimes.com/2018/06/05/opinion/qatar-blockade-foreign-minister.html.

and the arbitration of disputes."¹ As a prerequisite, parties to this and future disputes would use the new framework to "agree on basic security principles and rules of governance, and at least a minimum level of security to allow for peace and prosperity." This would be followed by the introduction of "binding arbitration mechanisms" that could be "enforced by the collective body of the region." The wider international community would provide diplomatic support and pressure to bolster this "holistic [regional] security agreement," as the Qatari leader termed his proposal.²

The GCC was initially established in 1981 in response to the Iranian revolution of 1979 and the start of the bitter, brutal and destructive eight-year war between Iran and Iraq that overshadowed the organization's first decade. Over the subsequent three decades, the GCC had a far-from-perfect record. Like all other ROs, its members regularly competed against each other, engaged in numerous squabbles and became embroiled in various political stand-offs. They also repeatedly demonstrated an unwillingness to cede national sovereignty in order to achieve deeper regional integration. This meant that even before the blockade began in mid-2017, the GCC was very far from functioning in a coherent fashion in the realms of finance, trade, defense and security. At the same time, local feuds and diverging national interests, as well as different operational capabilities and threat perceptions prevented GCC member states from developing a united and consistent policy approach in the military and security spheres.

The move toward a truly collective regional security framework was also hampered by the unwillingness of a majority of member states—the UAE, Oman and Kuwait, as well as Qatar—to participate in any GCC security agreement that might formalize the dominance of Saudi Arabia, the grouping's biggest military and economic player. Only Bahrain, for

---

1 "Speech of Qatar Emir at Munich Security Conference," *The Peninsula*, February 16, 2018 (Accessed, March 12, 2021)
   https://thepeninsulaqatar.com/article/16/02/2018/Speech-of-Qatar-Emir-at-Munich-Security-Conference.
2 For a detailed examination of these proposals see Rory Miller, "Managing Regional Conflict: The Gulf Cooperation Council and the Embargo of Qatar," *Global Policy* 10, no. 2 (June 2019): 36–45.

example, openly backed the Riyadh Declaration of 2011, the Saudi proposal for the GCC to be transformed into a fully-fledged union with a joint GCC military command.[1]

At the same time, the GCC provided an important framework for member states to put their grievances and national ambitions on hold and chisel out a united response in the political, economic and military realms at moments of regional crisis. This was demonstrated in their response to the Iraqi invasion of Kuwait in 1990 and the American invasion of Iraq in 2003. It was also evident during the crucial months of the Arab Spring in the first half of 2011. As much of the Arab world descended into chaos, the GCC states acted with composure and cemented their status as the key Arab powerbrokers in a period of flux. Member states also did an impressive job in using the GCC as a mechanism to prevent the militarization of their differences with each other beyond localized and irregular clashes.

To take one recent example. On coming to power in the summer of 2013, Qatar's new Amir, H.H. Sheikh Tamim bin Hamad Al-Thani, demonstrated a willingness to heal the rift between his kingdom and Saudi Arabia that had defined the relationship during much of the previous two decades. He visited Riyadh to meet bilaterally with the Saudi king and made a commitment to avoid any actions that damaged the interests of his GCC partners or destabilized the Gulf region. In the immediate term these moves did little to mitigate tensions. In March 2014, Saudi Arabia, the UAE and Bahrain recalled their ambassadors from Doha and all three countries threatened to implement sanctions against Qatar.

The unprecedented and coordinated diplomatic boycott of 2014 was intended to send a clear message to Doha that those of its policies that contradicted the interests of its GCC partners would no longer be tolerated. Relations continued to be strained until mid-November 2014 when GCC leaders attended an unannounced and impromptu meeting in Saudi Arabia dedicated to using multiparty negotiations to overcome internal differences. This was followed the next day by a phone

---

1   "Saudi King Abdullah Urges GCC 'To Move from Phase of Cooperation to Phase of Union," *Al Arabiya*, December 20, 2011 (Accessed May 2, 2020) https://www.alarabiya.net/articles/2011/12/20/183512.html.

conversation between the rulers of Saudi Arabia and Qatar that opened the way for a new beginning at the thirty-fifth annual GCC leaders' summit in Doha the following month.

This meeting was not without disagreement but outstanding concerns aside, all attending worked hard to foster improved relations and cooperation, if not harmony, on a range of issues. Qatar's then foreign minister H.E. Dr. Khalid bin Mohamed Al-Attiyah even briefed journalists that intra-GCC differences were "something from the past now."[1] This incident, which foreshadowed the current crisis, was resolved through a mixture of mediated, bilateral and multiparty negotiations inside the GCC that succeeded, in the short term at least, in ending a potentially major crisis.

In these terms, the GCC, for all its faults, was a ground-breaking and precedent-setting regional institution in both the Middle East and wider developing world.[2] Yet with the start of the blockade in early June 2017, Qatar's foreign minister, H.E. Sheikh Mohammed bin Abdulrahman Al-Thani, warned that there now existed "a big question mark"[3] over the GCC's future. Subsequently, other senior figures, notably Kuwait's Amir, Sheikh Sabah Al-Ahmad Al-Sabah, the most active local mediator in the crisis, acknowledged the same.[4]

While the GCC continues to function on paper at least, the recently resolved crisis has greatly complicated the efforts of member states to work together to expand inter-regional trade, attract more foreign investment, and achieve greater economies of scale and improved competitiveness. The blockade also greatly complicated efforts to develop

---

1 *Kuwait News Agency*, November 25, 2014.
2 Zeev Maoz, "Domestic Politics of Regional Security: Theoretical Perspectives and Middle East Patterns," *Journal of Strategic Studies* 26, no. 3 (2010): 19–48. Gavin Cawthra, "Collaborative Regional Security and Mutual Defence: SADC in Comparative Perspective," *Politikon* 35, no. 2 (2008): 159–176.
3 "Qatar FM: Question Mark Over Future of GCC After Crisis," *Al Jazeera*, June 6, 2017 (Accessed May 20, 2020) https://www.aljazeera.com/news/2017/06/qatar-fm-question-mark-future-gcc-crisis-170606001033685.html.
4 "Kuwait Emir Warns of GCC Collapse and Crisis Escalation," *Al Jazeera*, October 27, 2017 (Accessed May 20, 2020) https://www.aljazeera.com/news/2017/10/kuwait-emir-warns-gcc-collapse-crisis-escalation-171024122229727.html.

security cooperation. This is especially the case in traditionally sensitive areas like counter-terrorism and intelligence sharing that rely on the trust generated by shared external threats and long-time bonds of co-operation.

Qatar's response to the blockade since June 2017 has challenged East's argument that small states are primarily reactive if not inactive political entities.[1] Similarly, the refusal of Qatari leaders to consider themselves constrained in their actions by the disparity in size their country faced in relation to the blockading coalition underscores the arguments in the literature that a state's self-perception of its size and environment is very subjective and can be an important determinant of how a small state acts in the international system.[2] From this perspective, Qatar's response to the blockade has repeatedly challenged Vital's famous dictum that "weakness" is the "most common, natural and pervasive view of *self* in the small state."[3]

In doing so, the Qatari experience during the blockade, in particular its demonstration of the ways that small states can find security opportunities in the contemporary international system, has further made the case for a more nuanced view of small state power. Indeed, Qatar's response to the blockade offers a very valuable contemporary case study for reconsidering the limits of small state power and resilience in the face of much larger and, on paper at least, much stronger opponents.

---

1 M. East, "Size and Foreign Policy Behavior: A Test for Two Models"; See also M. East, S. Salmore and C. Hermann, *Why Nations Act* (Beverly Hills: Sage, 1978).
2 A. K. Henrikson, "A Coming 'Magnesian' Age? Small States, the Global System, and the International Community," *Geopolitics* 6, no.2 (2001): 49–86; M. Papadakis and H. Starr, "Opportunity, Willingness, and Small States: The Relationship Between Environment and Foreign Policy," in *New Directions in the Study of Foreign Policy*, eds, C. F. Hermann, C. W. Kegley, J. Rosenau (Boston: Allen & Unwin, 1987), 409–432.
3 David Vital, *The Inequality of Small States* (Oxford: Clarendon Press, 1967), 33.

CHAPTER 7

The Blockade of Qatar: Small States, Economic Development and National Resources

As a small state of 4,416 square miles with a population of 2.6 million, of whom more than 88 percent are non-citizens, the issue of Qatar's economic development and national resources in the context of the 2017 blockade of the country are intertwined in complex ways with its smallness.[1] This complexity emanates from the idea of national resources as tangible and intangible instruments of power, which according to Bridge can be a cultural mediation of the physical environment in addition to being shaped by factors such as the economy, political institutions, social attributes and belief systems.[2] Moreover, the essence of Qatar is not simply its fixed size,[3] to borrow Thorhallsson's phrase, but the interrelationship between vulnerability and resilience in terms of economics, political-economy, international relations and domestic policies.

It is for this reason that Long argues with regards to the categorization of small states that "quantification's intuitive appeal is undermined by

---

1   Jure Snoj, "Population of Qatar by Nationality—2017 Report," Priya Dsouza Communications, Doha, August 15, 2019, no. 2 https://priyadsouza.com/population-of-qatar-by-nationality-in-2017/.
2   Gavin Bridge, "Resource Geography," in *International Encyclopaedia of Social and Behavioural Sciences*, eds.
    Neil J. Smelser and Paul B. Baltes (Oxford: Pergamon, 2001): 1326–1329.
3   Baldur Thorhallsson, "The Size of States in the European Union: Theoretical and Conceptual Perspective," *Journal of European Integration* 28, no. 1 (2006): 7–31.

seemingly arbitrary numerical cut-offs."[1] Nor are small states like Qatar necessarily helpless even when power is considered in the context of material, especially economic, capabilities. This is because small states can possess and produce crucial resources, such as liquefied natural gas (LNG) in Qatar's case, which can serve as the basis of power. Additionally, the intangible economic or natural resources of small states can be linked to Thorhallsson's ideas of perceptual size and preference size.[2]

The blockade of Qatar can be understood and analyzed in terms of small state resources as both tangible and intangible phenomena and in terms of the vulnerability/resilience paradigm of economic development. This final chapter seeks, therefore, to develop an understanding of how Qatar as a small state used its national resources and economic development as leverage in circumventing and resisting the Saudi-led blockade between mid-2017 and early 2021.

Qatar's Leadership and Vision

Although the vulnerabilities of a small state like Qatar are, in conceptual terms at least, detrimental to its economic power, Briguglio has shown that some small states with vulnerable economies leverage their location and develop policy competencies that lead to the achievement of economic success. This "Singapore paradox,"[3] as referred to in previous chapters, has been a key factor in the successful leadership and vision of Singapore's founding father Lee Kuan Yew and his successors.

Quah argues that there are five reasons why Singapore has transformed itself so successfully from a small fishing village into a world-class modern

---

1 Tom Long, "Small States, Great Power? Gaining Influence Through Intrinsic, Derivative and Collective Power," *International Studies Review* 19, no.2 (2017): 185–205.
2 Baldur Thorhallsson, "The Size of States in the European Union: Theoretical and Conceptual Perspectives," *Journal of European Integration* 28, no. 1 (2006): 7–31.
3 Lino Briguglio, "Economic Vulnerability and Resilience: Concepts and Measurements," in *Vulnerability and Resilience of Small States*, eds. L. Briguglio and E. J. Kisanga (London, Commonwealth Secretariat and the University of Malta, 2004), 43–53.

city: pragmatic leadership, effective public bureaucracy, effective control of corruption, investment in education, competitive compensation, and learning from other countries.[1] The importance of the agency of leaders is that it enables the overcoming of larger constraints as Richard J. Samuels succinctly argues: Leaders play an important role in "stretching" the constraints of "geography and natural resources, institutional legacies and international locations."[2]

Equally important to the development of Qatar's resilience in the face of its inherent vulnerabilities has been its leadership. Cavusoglu argues that, "Political leadership is a dynamic and multidimensional conception in which historical, geographical, social, institutional and structural factors are taken into account besides the traits and personality of a leader."[3] This is underscored by the exposition of Mascuili et al. on the characteristics of an effective leader as strategic, tactical and innovatively adaptive.[4] These leadership characteristics make possible the delivery of successful outcomes. As the previous chapter on Qatar's foreign policy and security response to the blockade noted, since gaining independence in 1971 and moving on from its status as a British protectorate, Qatar has had a turbulent relationship with Saudi Arabia, initially because of a territorial dispute that resulted in Qatar suspending the 1965 border agreement between the two countries.

These tensions have been especially pronounced since June 1995 when H.H. Sheikh Hamad bin Khalifa Al-Thani replaced H.H. Sheikh Khalifa bin Hamad Al-Thani as Qatar's new leader.[5] The new Amir, with the

---

1   Jon S.T. Quah, "Why Singapore Works: Five Secrets of Singapore's Success," *Public Administration and Policy* 21, no. 1 (2018): 5–21.
2   Richard J. Samuels, *Machiavelli's Children: Leaders and Their Legacies in Italy and Japan* (Ithaca, NY, Cornell University Press, 2003), 1–2.
3   Esra Cavusoglu, "From Rise to Crisis: The Qatari Leadership," *Turkish Journal of Middle Eastern Studies* 7, no. 1 (2020): 81–109.
4   Joseph Mascuili, Milkhail A. Molchaov and W. Andy Knight, "Political Leadership in the Context," in *The Ashgate Research Companion to Political Leadership*, ed. Milkhail A. Molchaov (Farnham, Ashgate, 2009), 2–26.
5   Andrew Hammond, *Qatar's Leadership Transition: Like Father, Like Son* (London, European Council on Foreign Relations, 2014). https://www.ecfr.eu/publications/summary/qatars_transition_like_father_like_son304.

support of influential family members who shared his rejection of Saudi hegemonic aspirations, embodied tactical, strategic and innovatively adaptive visionary leadership that has continued under his son H.H. Sheikh Tamim bin Hamad Al-Thani since his father's abdication in 2013.[1]

The attempts, by both father and son, to develop Qatar's capabilities independently on both the domestic and international levels have proven contentious for Saudi Arabia. The June 2017 blockade of Qatar was the culmination of these tensions that were fueled further by Saudi Arabia's ambition to be a dominant regional hegemon and Qatar's desire for autonomy and a "robust leadership role within the Arab League."[2] Qatar's significant energy resources, its relationship with the US, Iran and Islamist groups such as the Muslim Brotherhood, and its media ambitions in the form of Al Jazeera have further exacerbated the turbulent relationship between Doha and Riyadh.[3]

Thorhallsson has argued that when considering the role of small states in geopolitics, it is important to explore international relations theories "that can provide simplified frameworks for interpreting the infinitely complex world of states, international organizations and other world actors."[4] In these terms, Morgenthau's theory of political realism provides an important explanation for the decisions of Qatari leaders in the safeguarding of their country's sovereignty. In his famous work, *Politics Among Nations: The Struggle for Power*, Morgenthau articulates the following principles: politics follows human nature and it is self-interested; it is also about the development of autonomy; self-interest is fundamental and changes with time; national security interests can lead to the

---

1 Ibid.
2 Sultan Barakat, *The Qatari Spring: Qatar's Emerging Role in Peacemaking* (London, LSE, 2012), 3; David B. Roberts, "Punching Above Its Weight: Could Tiny Qatar Send Ground Forces to Libya?," *Foreign Policy*, April 12, 2012 (Accessed May 20, 2020) https://foreignpolicy.com/2011/04/12/punching-above-its-weight-2/.
3 Abdul Rezak Bilgin, "Relations Between Qatar and Saudi Arabia After the Arab Spring," *Contemporary Arab Affairs* 11, no. 3 (2018): 113–134.
4 Baldur Thorhallsson, "Studying Small States: A Review," *Small States & Territories* 1, no. 1 (2018): 17–34.

infringement of private ethics; and state activity is broad and requires awareness of "human restrictions and incompetence."[1]

It is for all these reasons that despite their common ancestry, religion, geography and history, Qatar's leaders have attempted to balance against Saudi Arabia's behavior over the last quarter of a century through the diversification of its alliances across the geopolitical system. Notably, as mentioned in the previous chapter, after the Saudis and their allies blockaded Qatar in 2017, Qatari leaders strengthened their pre-existing relationships with Iran and Turkey. As Cavusoglu notes, this underscores the way that Qatar "quickly adopted a strategic approach to transform challenging circumstances into advantages."[2] As the remainder of this chapter will discuss and examine, central to this was the way that the Qatari leadership accessed and deployed the country's national resources.

National Resources in the Qatari Context

In the conceptualization of small states' national resources, the tendency is to focus on material resources that underscore the tools of power in the realist paradigm. The discussion in chapter 3 explained how these resources can be either tangible or intangible. For a small state like Qatar, an abundance of material resources does not necessarily guarantee the autonomy that it seeks to project. It is in this context that Cherkaoui, in referring to Qatar's US$130,000 annual per capita income,[3] argues that "Being an affluent yet small state is a dangerous prospect in the Middle East."[4] This supports the argument of Keohane and others that the structural vulnerabilities of small states makes them "more preoccupied than bigger actors with immediate security concerns and their own

---

1   Abdul Rezak Bilgin, "Relations Between Qatar and Saudi Arabia After the Arab Spring," 116.
2   Esra Cavusoglu, "From Rise to Crisis: The Qatari Leadership," 101.
3   Marc Champion, "Saudi Dispute with Qatar Has 22-Year History Rooted in Gas," *Bloomberg*, June 6, 2017 (Accessed May 21, 2020) https://www.bloomberg.com/news/articles/2017-06-06/saudi-arabia-s-feud-with-qatar-has-22-year-history-rooted-in-gas.
4   Tarek Cherkaoui, "Qatar's Public Diplomacy, International Broadcasting and the Gulf Crisis," *Rising Powers Quarterly* 3, no. 3 (2018): 129–149.

survival."[1] This preoccupation is certainly true for Qatar and underscores why it has used its vast natural gas resources in ways that strengthen its independence and sovereignty. It also reminds us that the possession of material resources like natural gas or other energy sources alone does not necessarily translate into regional or geopolitical security, never mind influence.

Long's argument about the complexity of power reminds us that in addition to natural resources, there is a need for structural, institutional and productive resources[2] if a small state wants to build the kind of resilience required to resist security challenges like the Saudi-led blockade that Qatar experienced. Therefore, while the argument holds true that the gas wealth of Qatar and its "surplus financial capabilities" have been crucial in enabling Qatar to stand up to its larger and more powerful neighbors,[3] Qatar's intangible resources have also played a salient role in this process. As the previous chapter noted, the Saudi-led blockading coalition was significantly larger in all traditional measures of power than Qatar. These differences underscore more recent arguments that move away from realist explanations for a small state's options in geopolitics and economics.

Nevertheless, Qatar's vast energy resources cannot be discounted in considering the development and enhancement of other tangible and intangible resources. This is why Miller alludes to the dual role of energy in Qatar's achievement of its internal and external priorities, as set out in its development roadmap, the Qatar National Vision 2030 (QNV) which was launched in 2008.[4] The essence of QNV is the recognition by Qatar that although the country has an abundance of hydrocarbons, especially natural gas (see Table 7.1), it is an exhaustible resource and the diversification of the country's resource base provides better long-term prospects for the country.

---

1 Robert Keohane, "Lilliputians' Dilemmas: Small States in International Politics," *International Organization* 23, no. 2 (Spring 1969): 291–310.
2 Tom Long, "Small States, Great Power? Gaining Influence Through Intrinsic, Derivative and Collective Power," 197.
3 Rory Miller, "Qatar, Energy Security, and Strategic Vision in a Small State," *Journal of Arabian Studies* 10, no. 1 (2020): 122–138.
4 Ibid, 124.

Table 7.1. Global Ranking of Natural Gas Exporters 2012

1	Russia	1,688,228,000	24.3%
2	Iran	1,201,382,000	17.3%
3	Qatar	871,585,000	12.5%
4	United States	368,704,000	5.3%
5	Saudi Arabia	294,205,000	4.2%
6	Turkmenistan	265,000,000	3.8%
7	United Arab Emirates	215,098,000	3.1%
8	Venezuela	197,087,000	2.8%
9	Nigeria	180,490,000	2.6%
10	China	163,959,000	2.4%

Source: BP Statistical Review of World Energy, 68th edition, 2019 (Accessed February 1, 2021) https://www.bp.com/content/dam/bp/business-sites/en/global/corporate/pdfs/energy-economics/statistical-review/bp-stats-review-2019-natural-gas.pdf; US Energy Information Administration, 'International,' https://www.eia.gov/international/overview/world.

Resource-based diversification requires that a state goes beyond narrow realism predicated on tangible material capabilities. That said, the strategic importance of Qatar's material resources in withstanding the 2017 blockade is evidenced by the increase in its liquid natural gas (LNG) production from 77 million tons to more than 100 million tons annually.[1] This is more than a 20 percent increase in Qatar's production capacity and Cavusoglu argues that the purpose was twofold: to improve its economic outcome and "to enlarge its exporting capacity and with it the Qatari impact on global energy markets."[2] With the UAE (one of the blockading countries) receiving around a third of its LNG needs from

---

1 Kristian Coates Ulrichsen, "Why Is Qatar Leaving OPEC?," *New York Times,* December 10, 2018 (Accessed May 18, 2020) https://www.nytimes.com/2018/12/10/opinion/qatar-leaving-opec-saudi-arabia-blockade-failure.html.
2 Esra Cavusoglu, "From Rise to Crisis: The Qatari Leadership," 103.

Qatar prior to the blockade,[1] this increase not only facilitated the needs of other countries for whom Qatar is a long-term supplier but also ensured the continuation of Qatar's supply to a hostile neighbor. Gloystein and Tay indicate that by ramping up its production, Qatar stood to increase its annual revenue by approximately US$30 billion with another US$6 billion being derived from condensate.[2] This strategic move by Qatar before and during the early stages of the crisis was a major factor in facilitating the country's stand against the Saudi-led coalition for the duration of the blockade.

Rende estimates that since the beginning of twenty-first century Qatar has spent around US$150 billion to make itself "the largest LNG producer and exporter in the world."[3] Qatar's strategic investment in its energy resources has been the bridge that spans the material resources of realist thought and the intangible resources of liberalism, institutionalism, constructivism, status seeking and sheltering. This underscores the argument that resources as a power base can be understood in the context of an asymmetric relationship[4] alongside relational power or weakness[5] and the quantitative or qualitative attributes of resources.[6] In other words, Qatar's ability to neutralize the effects of the blockade imposed by its Arab neighbors has been successful, not only because it has strategically

---

1. Jane Kinninmont, *The Gulf Divided – The Impact of the Qatari Crisis* (London: Chatham House, 2019). https://www.chathamhouse.org/publication/gulf-divided-impact-qatar-crisis.
2. Henning Gloystein and Mark Tay, "Qatar Signals LNG Price War for Market Share in Asia," *Reuters*, July 5, 2017 (Accessed May 18, 2020) https://www.reuters.com/article/us-qatar-lng/qatar-signals-lng-price-war-for-market-share-in-asia-idUSKBN19Q0YX.
3. Mithat Rende, "The Qatar Diplomatic Crisis and the Politics of Energy," *Turkish Policy Quarterly* 16, no. 2, (2017): 60–64.
4. Tom Long, "Small States, Great Power? Gaining Influence Through Intrinsic, Derivative and Collective Power," 187.
5. Mathias Maass, "The Elusive Definition of the Small State," *International Politics* 46, no. 1 (2009): 65–83.
6. Tom Rostoks, "Small States, Power, International Change and the Impact of Uncertainty', in *Small States in Europe: Challenges and Opportunities*, eds. Robert Steinmetz and Anders Wivel (Farnham, Ashgate, 2010), 87–101.

deployed its material resources, but also because it has deployed its non-material resources.

From the liberal perspective, the non-material resources of Qatar can be viewed in terms of the three assumptions set down by Moravcsik and discussed in chapter 2. The first of these assumptions provides the foundational basis of international law based on Locke's liberal individualism. For the leaders of Qatar, international law provides a resource in resisting the blockade. For example, Rossi refers to Qatar taking the UAE to the International Court of Justice (ICJ) in regard to Article 36 of the Statue with respect to the violation of the International Convention on the Elimination of All Forms of Racial Discrimination (CERD) to which the two states are signatories. As one legal commentator noted, in this case Qatar "accused the UAE of targeting Qataris based on their national origin, in violation of CERD's prohibition against racial discrimination."[1]

Qatar also took the blockading states to task over their violation of the Convention on International Civil Aviation (also known as the Chicago Convention), which requires signatories (including the four key members of the blockading coalition) to allow charter aircraft to "enter or transit through the airspace of a signatory state without obtaining prior authorization."[2] Qatar was also able to challenge the legal basis of the blockade due to the absence of a UN Security Council resolution authorizing sanctions against the country.[3] By using international law as an instrument, Qatar effectively challenged a quartet with a far greater combined GDP, physical size, population and military.

Qatar was also able to resist effectively the blockade in line with Moravcsik's second assumption on liberalism, which is consistent with constituency interests, for which Beckley's conceptualization indicates

---

[1] Christopher R. Rossi, "Game of Thornes: The Qatar Crisis, Forced Expulsion on the Arabian Peninsula," *Penn State Journal of Law & International Affairs* 7, no. 1 (2019): 1–52.

[2] Chiara Giuliani, *The Intra-GCC Crisis: Qatari Soft Power and International Law*, Rome, Instituto Affari Internazionali, 2019. https://www.iai.it/en/pubblicazioni/intra-gcc-crisis-qatari-soft-power-and-international-law.

[3] Ibid.

power in terms of outcomes.¹ For Qatari leaders, this crisis was a test of their resolve to protect the sovereignty of their small state as well as its autonomy. This resolve means that after the initial shock of the blockade and the issuing of the Saudi-led coalition's thirteen demands,² the Qatar leadership used its power to realize solutions to the blockade that were in the interests of domestic constituencies: national pride, the defense of sovereignty and resistance to Saudi hegemony. In these terms, power, for Qatar, was an outcome of autonomy based on grit, luck and wisdom (knowledge), as espoused by Beckley.³

The Amir of Qatar, H.H. Sheikh Tamim bin Hamad Al-Thani, did not concede to the demands of the quartet. As he told an audience at the UN: "We have refused to yield to dictation by pressure and blockade, and our people will not be satisfied with anything less."⁴ Instead, at various international fora, he proposed "a broader platform for dialogue and negotiation, invoking a framework for regional governance and the arbitration of disputes, modeled on that used by the EU to achieve the peaceful resolution of intra-RO tensions and 'establish shared security based on mutual interests ....'"⁵ Beyond this, in order to ensure the mutual security and dignity of the people of the wider Gulf region, the Qatari leadership sought outcomes not only beneficial for its own citizens and residents but also for the people of the blockading states.

Equally important as a resource that underscored Qatar's determination to resist the blockade is Moravcsik's third assumption about liberalism which emphasizes international cooperation. This can be linked to Thorhallsson's categorization of preference size and perceptual size for

---

1   Michael Beckley, "The Power of Nations, Measuring What Matters," *International Security* 43, no. 3 (2018): 7–44.
2   Rory Miller, "Managing Regional Conflict: The Gulf Cooperation Council and the Embargo of Qatar," *Global Policy* 10, no. 2 (2019): 36–45.
3   Michael Beckley, "The Power of Nations, Measuring What Matters," 13.
4   Address by His Highness Sheikh Tamim bin Hamad Al-Thani, Amir of the State of Qatar, New York, UN General Assembly, September 19, 2017, 17–21. https://www.qatar-tribune.com/Latest-News/ArtMID/423/ArticleID/25493/Amir-to-address-UN-general-assembly-in-New-York-tomorrow.
5   Ibid.

small states as well as Long's collective power paradigm in regard to small states. Qatar ensured that its relationships with Iran and Turkey were strengthened, especially given that the blockade by land, sea and air raised the risk of food and other commodity shortages and challenged the continued functioning of Qatar Airways.

In his public statements, Qatar's Amir also acknowledged how his country "participated in international coalitions and regional organizations and nurtured bilateral relations with the United States of America and many countries of the world." This use of international cooperation as a resource to counter the negative impact of the blockade has been made possible, to a significant extent, by Qatar's global trade relationship and its interconnected strategic exploitation of its energy resources.

The nexus between Qatar's international cooperation and its resources can also be understood in institutional terms. Jonsson and Tallberg argue that rational choice institutionalism presents opportunities for states to take advantage of collectivism, interdependence and strategic interaction.[1] This resonates with the Qatari leader's call at the 2018 Munich Security Conference for "dialogue and negotiation" among regional actors as well as intra-regional organizations.[2] At the UN General Assembly in 2019, Amir Al-Thani followed this up by noting his country's "commitment to multilateral international action, partnership and cooperation for the interest of our peoples and the good of humanity."[3]

Qatar, therefore, viewed the resource role of the UN, the GCC, the ICJ and other international organizations as salient parts of its armory in resisting the potentially crippling blockade imposed by the quartet. Katzenstein argues that small European countries joined the EU not only for interdependence, strategic interaction and collective action but also to

---

1   Christer Jönsson and Jonas Tallberg, *Institutional Theory in International Relations* (Lund: Lund University, 2001). https://portal.research.lu.se/portal/files/6355177/625444.pdf.

2   Rory Miller, "Managing Regional Conflict: Gulf Cooperation Council and the Embargo of Qatar," 40.

3   "Only International Actions Can Settle the World's 'Enormous and Diverse Cross-Border Challenges,' Qatar Tells UN Assembly," September 24, 2019, *UN News* (Accessed May 18, 2020) https://news.un.org/en/story/2019/09/1047282.

restrain the hegemony of bigger powers. Qatar's active role in the UN and its efforts to develop new ROs are intended to serve the same purpose for this small state.

Constructivism, which Dormer argues entails concepts such as intersubjectivity, identity, beliefs, norms and agency, also helps us understand more clearly Qatar's attempts to oppose the blockade.[1] Such concepts have enabled Qatar to sustain, as well as develop, a separate identity, even though the ruling Al-Thani family originated from the Najd region of Saudi Arabia which is the birthplace of Wahhabism, the dominant Muslim belief of Saudi Arabia.

Cavusoglu argues that Qatar's interpretation of Wahhabism is substantially different from that of the Saudis. This difference is demonstrated through Qatari moderation which provides, for example, long-time support for, among other things, a woman's right to drive, travel and participate in municipal elections.[2] Qatari women, including H.H. Sheikha Moza bint Nasser who is the chairperson of Qatar Foundation (QF), have been prominent in advocating increased education opportunities for females.[3] This can be linked to Ulrichsen's point about the role of Qatar's state brand in promoting the country as a "neutral and progressive leader within the Arab and Islamic world, and to garner the support of the wider Arab region in addition to the broader international community."[4] This branding includes developing Qatar into a knowledge hub for "educational, scientific and cultural projects …,"[5] all of which have been made possible by utilizing Qatar's bridge—its energy resources—in the service of developing social resources.

---

1 Robert Dormer, "The Impact of Constructivism on International Relations Theory: A History," *Kwansei Gakuin University Social Science Review* 22, (2017): 51–64.
2 Esra Cavusoglu, "From Rise to Crisis: The Qatari Leadership," 93.
3 Paul Michael Brannagan and Richard Giulianotti, "The Soft Power—Soft Disempowerment Nexus: The Case of Qatar," *International Affairs* 94, no. 5 (2018): 1139–1157.
4 Kristian Coates Ulrichsen, *Qatar and the Arab Spring* (London: Hurst, 2014), 38.
5 Tarek Cherkaoui, "Qatar's Public Diplomacy, International Broadcasting and the Gulf Crisis," 131.

In conjunction with the constructivist paradigm, small states like Qatar also employ status seeking strategies as resources in their international engagement. Wohlforth et al. argue that small states do this "by taking on admirable tasks or excelling in a particular field."[1] An example of a status seeking resource for Qatar is what Miller and Verhoeven refer to as "the Al Jazeera Effect," which is not limited to global broadcasting but the Qatar Foundation and Education City with a number of Western universities including those from the US, the UK and France.[2]

As the previous chapter noted, Qatar has also sought status via conflict mediation in places like Yemen, Lebanon, Chad, Sudan and Afghanistan among others. Brannagan and Giulianotti have argued that status seeking achievements can lead to disempowerment for small states as other actors become envious.[3] Despite this challenge, Qatar used status as a currency in its attempts to resist the blockade. On top of winning the right to host the FIFA World Cup in 2022, Qatar's sporting diplomacy has also provided the status required to influence the international system. This has included the hosting of the fifteenth Asian Games in 2006, sponsorship of FC Barcelona in Spain, hosting the ATP Tennis tour in Doha, in addition to the purchase of the French football team Paris Saint-Germain.[4]

Qatar's Economic Development and the Blockade

The vulnerability/resilience dichotomy of a small state economy is evident even in a resource-rich country like Qatar. This is why Vital argues that "the smaller the human and material resources of a state, the greater are the difficulties it must surmount if it is to maintain any valid political options at all."[5] Qatar has used its economic development to

---

1 Baldur Thorhallsson, "Studying Small States: A Review," 26.
2 Rory Miller and Harry Verhoeven, "Overcoming Smallness: Qatar, the United Arab Emirates and Strategic Realignment in the Gulf," *International Politics* 57, no. 1 (February 2020): 1–20.
3 Paul Michael Brannagan and Richard Giulianotti, "The Soft Power – Soft Disempowerment Nexus: The Case of Qatar," 1152.
4 Tarek Cherkaoui, "Qatar's Public Diplomacy, International Broadcasting and the Gulf Crisis," 132–133.
5 David Vital, *The Inequality of Small States* ((Oxford: Clarendon Press, 1967), 3.

avoid the problems noted by Vital, primarily through its evolution into a strategic energy actor.[1] This has involved the transition from a secondary oil producer to a global gas giant and then a transition from an ordinary upstream producer of natural gas to a downstream producer as part of a move toward a diversified economic base.

In seeking to provide an analysis of the dichotomous attributes of small state economics, Briguglio argues that there are three commonalities: A high degree of openness due to export and import dependency; a high concentration of exports due to the small size of the economy; and a disproportionate dependence on strategic imports including fuel and food.[2] The International Monetary Fund (IMF) reports that the Qatari economy has weathered these challenges, as well as the storm of low hydrocarbon prices since 2014 and the Saudi-led blockade, by utilizing strong buffers that include highly capitalized banks with a liquid-asset-to-total-asset ratio of 29.7 percent.[3]

The IMF has also noted how, despite the blockade, the Qatari economy boasts strong financial stability and that the "financial sector remains sound, underpinned by strong profitability and capital." Additionally, real GDP growth is expected to be stronger in the near term, although this is strengthened "by recovery in the hydrocarbon output" with medium-term growth being "buoyed by increased gas production and non-hydrocarbon growth."[4]

The centrality of hydrocarbon exports in the Qatari economy and the importation of the technology and technical-expertise required for exploration and resource production underscores Briguglio's small state export/import dependency argument, as does the concentration of exports due to the small size of Qatar's economy. The third argument relating to the import of essential goods also holds true for Qatar given that it has a

---

1   Rory Miller, "Qatar: Energy, Security, and Strategic Vision in a Small State," 124.
2   Lino Briguglio, "A Vulnerability and Resilience Framework for Small States', in *Building the Resilience of Small States: A Revised Framework*, ed. D. Bynoe-Lewis (London: Commonwealth Secretariat, 2014), 1–102.
3   International Monetary Fund, *Qatar – 2019 Article IV Consultation – Press Release, Staff Report*, IMF, Washington, DC, 2019.
4   Ibid, 1.

very low level of self-sufficiency in foodstuffs[1] (see Figure 7.1). Figure 7.2 also provides a possible reason why the Saudis and Emiratis were at the forefront of the blockade given that they were Qatar's top sources of food imports between 1998 and 2017.[2] However, while the blockade initially led to rising food shortages and associated national security challenges, it ultimately prompted Qatar to refocus its efforts on the diversification of its imports and domestic capacity, including improved food security. As noted above, the blockade also led to an acceleration of the strategy to increase LNG production.[3]

Figure 7.1. Qatari Food Self-Sufficiency 2016

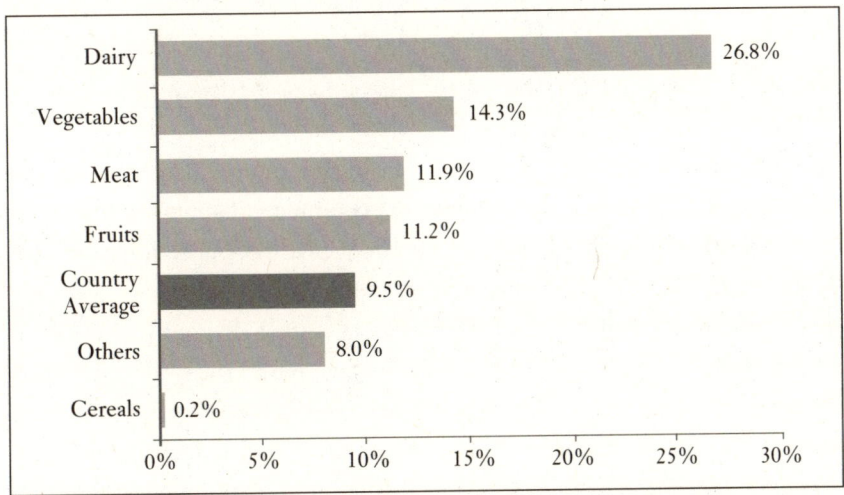

Source: Alpen Capital, *GCC Food Industry*, Alpen Capital, Abu Dhabi, 2019, https://argaamplus.s3.amazonaws.com/abcb9f47-79d3-4c4f-87a0-9a1188c7bc4e.pdf.

---

1   Alpen Capital, *GCC Food Industry*, Alpen Capital, Abu Dhabi, 2019, https://argaamplus.s3.amazonaws.com/abcb9f47-79d3-4c4f-87a0-9a1188c7bc4e.pdf.
2   Hela Miniaoui, Patrick Irungu and Simeon Kaitibie, "Contemporary Issues in Qatar's Food Security," *Middle East Insights* 185, (2018): 1–14.
3   Esra Cavusoglu, "From Rise to Crisis: The Qatari Leadership," 101.

Figure 7.2. Top 10 Sources of Food for Qatar 1998–2017

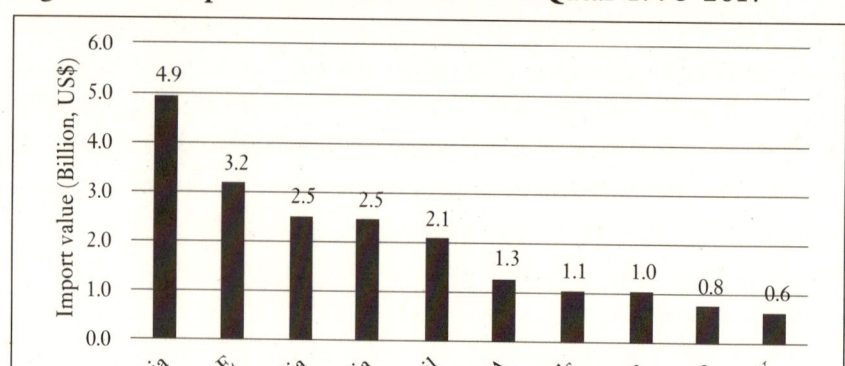

Source: Hela Miniaoui, Patrick Irungu and Simeon Kaitibie, "Contemporary Issues in Qatar's Food Security," *Middle East Insights* 185, (2018): 1–14.

With Qatar's energy sector still accounting for approximately 85 percent of government revenues, the question of economic vulnerability remains a pressing concern in regard to the economic security of the country. Indeed, while Qatar has been able to strategically deploy the resources of its energy sector to counter the impact of the blockade, any challenges that threaten its ability to sell these resources could adversely affect the economy.[1] Such concerns explain Payne's argument that even economically successful small states face the challenge of fundamentally adapting their intrinsically vulnerable characteristics.[2] Linked to this point, in exploring the question of whether resilience-building is triggered automatically or is a matter of choice in small economies, Briguglio distinguishes between causes and effects. He argues that it is possible to create policies that develop resilience-building, leading to the mitigation of vulnerabilities.[3]

---

1 Rory Miller, "Qatar: Energy Security, and Strategic Vision in a Small State," 133.
2 Antony Payne, "Afterword: Vulnerability as a Condition, Resilience as a Strategy" in *The Diplomacies of Small States: Between Vulnerability and Resilience*, eds. A.F. Cooper and T.M. Shaw (Basingstoke, Palgrave MacMillan, 2009), 279–286.
3 Lino Briguglio, "A Vulnerability and Resilience Framework for Small States', in *Building the Resilience of Small States: A Revised Framework*, ed. D. Bynoe-Lewis (London: Commonwealth Secretariat 2014), 10.

Qatar's leadership has been strategic in introducing policies that have given the economy both the flexibility and structure that allows for adaptability and the capacity to rebound from shocks. Through its public diplomacy, Qatar has been able to maintain the US CENTCOM base along with Turkish bases while continuing its economic activities with Iran.[1] These relationships have enabled Qatar to consolidate its physical security, as did the import of essential goods from Turkey and Iran, and the use of Iranian air space during the early days of the blockade.

Qatar continues its LNG trade with the UAE, despite the latter's role in the blockade, and its long-term LNG supply contracts in Europe, Asia and across the globe continued unabated for the duration of the blockade.[2] Qatar's sovereign wealth fund which is also one of the largest in the world with investments in many blue-chip firms including Porsche, Volkswagen, Siemens, Deutsche Bank, the London Stock Exchange, Barclays, Total and Orange S.A. (formerly France Télécom S.A.)[3] among others, has contributed to the ongoing Qatari diversification project. However, due to the small size of the domestic economy, diversification within Qatar in sectors including financial services, construction and manufacturing, though growing, still constitutes only a small fraction of government revenues in comparison to the energy sector.

Cooper and Shaw argue that economic resilience in a small state requires stability, good governance, efficiency and social development, especially if the state in question desires to influence the international system.[4] Social development is the fabric of the Qatar National Vision (QNV) 2030. The first two pillars of QNV 2030 are human development

---

1 Tarek Cherkaoui, "Qatar's Public Diplomacy, International Broadcasting and the Gulf Crisis," 139.

2 Paul Cochrane, "Supertanker State: How Qatar is Gambling Its Future on Global Gas Dominance," *Middle East Eye*, July 2, 2020 (Accessed July 10, 2020) https://www.middleeasteye.net/news/qatar-gas-lng-market-oil-prices-dominance.

3 Tarek Cherkaoui, "Qatar's Public Diplomacy, International Broadcasting and the Gulf Crisis," 132–133.

4 Antony F. Cooper and Timothy M. Shaw "The Diplomacies of Small States at the Start of the Twenty-First Century: How Vulnerable? How Resilient?," in *The Diplomacies of Small States: Between Vulnerabilities and Resilience*, eds. A.F. Cooper and T.M. Shaw (Basingstoke, Palgrave MacMillan, 2009), 1–18.

and social development, while the last two are economic development and environmental development.¹ QNV 2030 and Qatar's Second National Development Strategy 2018–2022 have focused on policies that facilitate resilience-building as well as good governance and efficient services.²

All this was evident when the Saudi-led blockade began in 2017. Qatar drew on its national resources and high levels of economic development to avoid economic crisis and prevent the undermining of its social fabric. These resources provided for the resilience, flexibility and structures required by leaders as part of their strategic vision. This enabled the country, a small state situated in a region in which larger neighbors and global powers engage in hegemonic posturing, to withstand the crisis for its duration.

Qatar's National Resources, Economic Development and the International System

Qatar's national resources (both material and non-material) were instrumental in the country's attempts to counter the blockade in order to protect its sovereignty at the same time as they have allowed it to continue to influence the international system. This has been made possible in part due to Qatar's control of the world's third-largest gas reserves which generate revenues of tens of billions of dollars annually. For example, Moody's estimated that between June and July 2017, Qatar spent at least US$38.5 billion of its reserves to ensure its economic autonomy and political independence.³

Qatar has also attempted to convert its material resources into non-material currencies. The country's soft power, which is built partly on public diplomacy, is underpinned by developing a state brand that is

---

1   General Secretariat for Development Planning, *Qatar National Vision 2030*, Doha, 2008. https://www.psa.gov.qa/en/qnv1/pages/default.aspx.

2   Ministry of Development, Planning, Statistics, *Qatar's Second National Development Strategy 2018–2022*, Doha, 2018.
https://www.psa.gov.qa/en/knowledge/Documents/NDS2Final.pdf.

3   Zahraa Akjgakisi, "Qatar Burns $38 Billion in Reserves as Boycott Bites," *CNN Business*, September, 14, 2017 (Accessed May 18, 2020) https://money.cnn.com/2017/09/14/news/economy/qatar-isolation-economy-reserves/index.html.

impactful across the international system. Al Jazeera, the Qatar Investment Authority (QIA), QatarEnergy, Qatar Foundation (QF), Education City, Qatar Airways, and the 2022 FIFA World Cup[1] have all contributed to Qatar's status in the international system and have helped it to maintain its economic autonomy and political independence in the years since the blockade began. It is also the case that during the blockade Qatar used its gas revenues as a "key part of its soft power arsenal." Doing so, as Miller argues, enabled it "to engage in financial diplomacy and to fund major deals with important external partners. In this process, the country has consolidated bilateral ties and persuaded actors across Europe, Africa and Asia to remain neutral".[2]

More generally, this point supports Vaicekauskaite's argument that despite the challenges that small states face, their influence in the international system can be predicated on the efficient and effective use of their material and non-material resources.[3] This is why, despite the vulnerability/resilience dichotomy of small states, building resilience not only involves achieving important macroeconomic benchmarks that bring stability but also the consolidation of more intangible factors like social development and good political governance. Cavusoglu argues that Qatar "realized a remarkable transformation at the domestic level through two major and concurrent achievements under Sheikh Hamad. The first one was the rapid economic and social development and modernization towards a knowledge-based economy .... The other equally significant achievement at the domestic level was the achievement of Qatar's political stability."[4]

Social development and political stability did indeed provide the bedrock of domestic Qatari support for the government in the face of the Saudi-led blockade and the capacity of Qatari leaders to speak, and be heard, at international fora. Therefore, despite the vulnerabilities that

---

1   Tarek Cherkaoui, "Qatar's Public Diplomacy, International Broadcasting and the Gulf Crisis," 127–149.
2   Rory Miller, "Qatar, Energy Security, and Strategic Vision in a Small State," 132.
3   Zivile Marija Vaicekauskaite, "Security Strategies of Small States," *Journal of Baltic Security* 3, no. 2 (2017): 7–15.
4   Esra Cavusoglu, "From Rise Crisis: The Qatari Leadership," 91.

Qatar faces as a small state, the stewardship of its national resources by its leadership and the support for economic development have provided the wherewithal for the country to consolidate its security and influence positively its position in the international system even as it resisted the blockade.

BIBLIOGRAPHY

Reports, Policy Papers and Official Documents

Aaltola, Mika, Joonas Sipilä, Valtteri Vuorisalo "Securing Global Commons: A Small State Perspective," The Finnish Institute of International Affairs, Working Paper 71, June 2011.

Acevedo, Sebastian, "Debt, Growth and Natural Disasters: A Caribbean Trilogy," IMF Working Paper No. 14/*125*, Washington DC, International Monetary Fund, 2014.

Al-Marri, Fahad, "The Impact COVID-19 has had on the Economic Growth Strategy of the GCC Countries and What Must Be Done." The Institute of Energy Economics, Japan (IEEJ), Working Paper, September 2021.

Al-Marri, Fahad, "The Impact of the Oil Crisis on Security and Foreign Policy in GCC Countries: Case Studies of Qatar, KSA and UAE." Research Paper, Arab Center for Research & Policy Studies, November 2017. https://www.dohainstitute.org/en/ResearchAndStudies/Pages/The-Impact-of-the-Oil-Crisis-on-Security-and-Foreign-Policy-in-GCC-Countries-Case-Studies-of-Qatar,-KSA-and-UAE.aspx.

Andreasson, Ulf, "Trust—the Nordic Gold." Copenhagen: Nordic Council of Ministers, 2017.

Briguglio, Lino, "Growth with Resilience: Perspective from the Commonwealth and Francophonie and Recommendation to the G20." London: Commonwealth Secretariat, 2011.

Briguglio, Lino, "A Vulnerability and Resilience Framework for Small States." London, Commonwealth Secretariat, 2014.

Commonwealth Secretariat, "Vulnerability: Small States in the Global Society." Report of a Commonwealth Consultative Group. London: Commonwealth Secretariat, 1985. https://www.thecommonwealth-ilibrary.org/commonwealth/economics/vulnerability_9781848593985-en.

Commonwealth Advisory Group, "A Future for Small States: Overcoming Vulnerability." London, Commonwealth Secretariat, 1997.

Commonwealth Secretariat/World Bank Joint Task Force, "Small States: Meeting Challenges in the Global Economy." Washington, DC: World Bank, 2000, http://documents.worldbank.org/curated/en/267231468763824990/Small-states-meeting-challenges-in-the-global-economy.

Cordina, Gordon, "The Macroeconomic and Growth Dynamics of Small States." Small

States: Economic Review & Basic Statistics, London: Commonwealth Secretariat, 2008.

Curmi, Liliana, "Governance and Small States." Occasional Papers on Islands and Small States, Valletta, Island and Small States Institute, University of Malta, 2009.

Foa, Roberto, "The Economic Rationale for Social Cohesion—The Cross-Country Evidence." International Conference on Social Cohesion, OECD, Paris, 2011.

General Secretariat for Development Planning, "Qatar National Vision 2030." 2008, https://www.psa.gov.qa/en/qnv1/pages/default.aspx.

Greenham, Tony, Elizabeth Cox and Josh Ryan-Collins, "Mapping Economic Resilience." York: Friends Provident Foundation, 2013.

Hallegatte, Stephane, "Economic Resilience—Definition and Measurement." Policy Research Working Paper 6852, Washington DC: The World Bank, 2014.

Haskins, Jeffery, "Building in Small Island Economies: from Vulnerabilities to Opportunities." CTA Policy Brief, 2012.

Hnatkovska, Viktoria V. and Norman Loayza, "Volatility and Growth." World Bank Policy Research Working Paper No. 3184, Washington DC: World Bank, 2004.

International Monetary Fund, "Macroeconomic Issues in Small States and Implications for Fund Engagement." Washington DC: IMF, 2013.

Kinninmont, Jane, "The Gulf Divided—The Impact of the Qatari Crisis." London: Chatham House, 2019. https://www.chathamhouse.org/publication/gulf-divided-impact-qatar-crisis.

Kraay, Aart and William Easterly, "Small States, Small Problems?" Policy Research Working Papers, Washington D.C: World Bank, 2007.

1999 https://elibrary.worldbank.org/doi/abs/10.1596/1813-9450-2139.

Lee, Dongyeol, Patrizia Tumbarello, Kazuaki Washimi and Tlek Zeinullayev, "Mind the Gap: Public Investment, Growth and Natural Disaster Risk in the Small States of the Pacific." Working Paper, Washington: International Monetary Fund, 2016.

Lewis-Bynoe, Denny, ed., "Building the Resilience of Small States: A Revised Framework." London: Commonwealth Secretariat, 2014.

Loayza, Norman V. and Raimundo Soto, "On the Measurement of Market-Oriented Reforms." Washington DC: World Bank, 2003.

Ulrichsen, Kristian Coates, "Small States With a Big Role: Qatar and the United Arab Emirates in the Wake of the Arab Spring." HH Sheikh Nasser al-Mohammad al-Sabah Publication Series, Durham: Durham University, 2012.

Vandemoortele, Milo, "Equity: A Key to Macroeconomic Stability." London: Overseas Development Institute, 2010.

World Bank, "The World Bank in Small States." https://www.worldbank.org/en/country/smallstates.

World Health Organization, "Special Initiative on Climate Change and Health in Small Island Developing States." World Health Organization: Geneva, 2011. https://www.who.int/news-room/detail/06-11-2017-special-initiative-on-climate-change-and-health-in-small-island-developing-states.

World Trade Organization, "Small Economies: A Literature Review." Geneva: Committee on Trade and Development, 2002. WT/COMTD/SE/W/4.

Yang, Yongzheng, Hong Chen, Shiuraj Singh and Baljeet Singh, "The Pacific Speed of Growth: How Fast Can It Be and What Determines It?" IMF working Paper, 13/104, Washington DC: IMF, 2013.

Books

Al-Ebraheem, Hassan Ali. *Kuwait and the Gulf: Small States and the International System*. 2nd ed. London: Routledge, 2016.

Balaam, David N. and Michael Veseth. *Introduction to International Political Economy*. Upper Saddle River, NJ: Prentice Hall, 1996.

Briguglio, Lino, Gordon Cordina, Stephanie Bugeja and Nadia Farrugia. *Conceptualising and Measuring Economic Resilience*. Valetta, University of Malta, 2006.

Carr, Edward H. *The Twenty Years' Crisis, 1919-1939: An Introduction to the Study of International Relations*. New York: Harper and Row, 1946.

Connell, John and Kristen Lowitt, eds. *Food Security in Small Island States*. Singapore: Springer Nature, 2020

Cooper, A. F. and T. M. Shaw, eds. *The Diplomacies of Small States: Between Vulnerability and Resilience*. Basingstoke: Palgrave MacMillan, 2009.

Cox, Robert W. and Timothy J. Sinclair. *Approaches to World Order*. Cambridge: Cambridge University Press, 1996.

Handel, Michael. *Weak States in the International System*. London: Frank Cass, 1981.

Hey, J. A. K, ed. *Small States in World Politics: Explaining Foreign Policy Behaviour*. Boulder, CO: Lynne Rienner, 2003.

Ingebritsen, Christine. *The Nordic States and European Unity*. Ithaca: Cornell University Press, 1998.

Ingebritsen, Christine, Iver B. Neumann, Sieglinde *Gstöhl, and Jessica Beyer*, eds. *Small States in International Relations*. University of Washington Press: Seattle, 2006.

Jarvis, Lee and Jack Holland. *Security: A Critical Introduction*. New York: Palgrave Macmillan, 2014.

Jonsson, Christer and Jonas Tallberg. *Institutional Theory in International Relations*. Lund: Lund University, 2001.

Kamrava, Mehran. *Qatar: Small State, Big Politics*. Ithaca: Cornell University Press, 2013.

Katzenstein, Peter J. *Small States in World Market: Industrial Policies in Europe*. Ithaca: Cornell University Press, 1985.

Lim, Timothy C. *International Political Economy: An Introduction to Approaches, Regimes and Issues*. Washington DC: Saylor Foundation, 2014.

Little, Richard. *The Balance of Power in International Relations: Metaphors, Myths and Models*. Cambridge: Cambridge University Press, 2007.

Miller, Rory, ed. *The Gulf Crisis: The View from Qatar*. Doha: Hamad bin Khalifa University Press, 2018.

Miller, Rory. *Desert Kingdoms to Global Powers: The Rise of the Arab Gulf*. New Haven: Yale University Press, 2016.

Morgenthau, Hans J. *Politics Among Nations: The Struggle for Power and Peace*. 3rd ed. Chicago: University of Chicago Press, 1948.

Ólafsson, Björn G. *Small States in Global System: Analysis and Illustrations from the Case of Iceland*. Ashgate, Aldershot, 1998.

Reid, G. L. *The Impact of Very Small Size on the International Relations Behavior of Microstates*. London: Sage, 1974.

Rosenau, James N. *Turbulence in World Politics: A Theory of Change and Continuity*. Princeton, New Jersey: Princeton University Press, 1990.

Rothstein, Robert L. *Alliances and Small Powers*. New York: Columbia University Press, 1968.

Sutch, Peter and Juanita Elias. *International Relations: The Basics*. New York: Routledge, 2007.

Thorhallsson, Baldur. *The Role of Small States in the European Union*. Burlington, VT: Ashgate Publishing Company, 2000.

Ulrichsen, Kristian Coates. *Qatar and the Arab Spring*. London: Hurst, 2014.

Viotti, Paul R. and Mark V. Kaupi. *International Relations Theory*. London: Longman Pearson, 2012.

Vital, David. *The Inequality of Small States*. Oxford: Clarendon Press, 1967.

Walt, Stephen. *The Origins of Alliances*. Ithaca: Cornell University Press, 1987.

Williams, P. D. and M. McDonald, eds. *Security Studies: An Introduction*. London/New York: Routledge 2018.

Articles

Adler, Emanuel and Patricia Greve. "When Security Community Meets Balance of Power: Overlapping Regional Mechanism of Security Governance." *Review of International Studies* 35, no. 1 (2009): 59–84.

Al-Ansari, Tareq. "Food Security: The Case of Qatar." In *The Gulf Crisis: The View from Qatar*, edited by Rory Miller, 28–38. Doha: Hamad bin Khalifa University Press, 2018.

Al-Marri, Fahad. "To What Extent Has the Sovereign Wealth Fund Assisted Qatar's Security and Foreign Policy in Resisting the Blockade?" In *The 2017 Gulf Crisis*, edited by Mahjoob Zweiri, Md Mizanur Rahman and Arwa Kamal.Vol 3, (2021): 303–324. Singapore: Springer.

Angstrom, Jan and Magnus Petersson. "Weak Party Escalation: An Underestimated Strategy for Small States?" *Journal of Strategic Studies* 42, no. 2 (2019): 282–300, 284–5.

Arreguin-Toft, Ivan. "How the Weak Win Wars: A Theory of Asymmetric Conflict." *International Security* 26, no. 1 (2001): 93–128.

Asutay, Mehmet. "GCC Sovereign Wealth Funds and Their Role in the European and American Markets." *Equilibri* 12, no. 3 (2008): 335–354.

Auty, Richard M. "Natural Resources and Small Island Economies: Mauritius and Trinidad and Tobago." *Journal of Development Studies* 53, no. 2 (2017): 264–277.

Baehr, Peter R. "Small States: A Tool for Analysis?" *World Politics* 27, no. 3 (1975): 456–466.

Bailes, Alyson J.K. and Baldur Thorhallsson. "Instrumentalizing the European Union in Small State Strategies." *Journal of European Integration* 35, no. 2 (2013): 99–115.

Bailes, Alyson J. K., Bradley A. Thayer and Baldur Thorhallsson. "Alliance Theory and

Alliance "Shelter": The Complexities of Small State Alliance Behaviour." *Third World Thematics: A TWQ Journal* 1, no. 1 (2016): 9–26.

Baldacchino, Godfrey. "The Contribution of "Social Capital" to Economic Growth: Lessons from Island Jurisdictions." *The Round Table: The Commonwealth Journal of International Affairs* 94, no. 378 (2005): 31–46.

Baldacchino, Godfrey and Geoff Bertram. "The Beak of the Finch: Insights into the Economic Development of Small Economies." *Round Table The Commonwealth Journal of International Affairs* 98, no. 401 (2009): 141–160.

Baldwin, David A. "Power and International Relations." In *Handbook of International Relations.* 2nd ed, edited by Walter Carlsnaes, Thomas Risse and Beth A. Simmons, London: Sage Publications, 2012.

Barnett, Michael and J. Levy. "Domestic Sources of Alliances and Alignments: The case of Egypt, 1962-1973." *International Organization* 45, no. 3 (1991): 369–395.

Barnett, Michael and Raymond Duvall. "Power in International Politics." *International Organisation* 59, no. 1 (2005): 39–75.

Bartmann, Barry. "Meeting the Needs of Microstate Security." *The Round Table: The Commonwealth Journal of International Affairs* 91, no. 365 (2002): 361–374.

Benwell, Richard. "The Canaries in the Coalmine: Small States as Climate Change Champions." *Round Table: The Commonwealth Journal of International Affairs* 100, no. 413 (2011): 199–211.

Bishop, Matthew L. "The Political Economy of Small States: Enduring Vulnerability?" *Review of International Political Economy* 19, no. 5 (2012): 942–960.

Björkdahl, Annika. "Norm Advocacy: A Small State Strategy to Influence the EU." *Journal of European Public Policy* 15, no. 1 (2008): 135–154.

―――― "Ideas and Norms in Swedish Peace Policy." *Swiss Political Science Review* 19, no. 3 (2013): 322–337.

Brannagan, Paul Michael and Richard Giulianotti. "The Soft Power–Soft Disempowerment Nexus: The Case of Qatar." *International Affairs* 94, no. 5 (2018): 1139–1157.

Braunstein, Juergen. "The Domestic Drivers of State Finance Institutions: Evidence from Sovereign Wealth Funds." *Review of International Political Economy* 26, no. 6 (2017): 980–1003.

Braveboy-Wagner, Jacqueline. "Opportunities and Limitations of the Exercise of Foreign Policy Power by a Very Small State: The Case of Trinidad and Tobago." *Cambridge Review of International Affairs* 23, no. 3 (2010): 407–427.

Briguglio, Lino. "Small Island States and Their Economic Vulnerabilities." *World Development* 23 (1995): 1615–1632.

―――― "Economic Vulnerability and Resilience: Concepts and Measurements." In *Vulnerability and Resilience of Small States*, edited by L. Briguglio and E.J. Kisanga, 43–53. London: Commonwealth Secretariat and the University of Malta, 2004.

Briguglio, Lino, Gordon Cordina, Nadia Farrugia and Stephanie Vella. "Economic Vulnerability and Resilience: Concepts and Measurements." *Oxford Development Studies* 37, no. 3 (2009): 229–247.

Broome, André. "Negotiating Crisis: The IMF and Disaster Capitalism in Small States."

The Round Table: The Commonwealth Journal of International Affairs,100, no. 413 (2011): 155–167.

Browning, Christopher. "Small, Smart and Salient? Rethinking Identity in the Small States Literature." *Cambridge Review of International Affairs*,19, no. 4 (2006): 669–684.

Burczynska, Maria E. "Multinational Cooperation: Building Capabilities in Small Air Forces." *European Security* 28, no. 1 (2019): 85–104.

Campbell, John L. and John A. Hall. "National Identity and the Political Economy of Small States." *Review of International Political Economy* 16, no. 4 (2009): 547–572.

Cavusoglu, Esra. "From Rise to Crisis: The Qatari Leadership." *Turkish Journal of Middle Eastern Studies* 7, no. 1 (2020): 81–109.

Cesnakas, Giedrius. "Energy Resources in Foreign Policy: A Theoretical Approach." *Baltic Journal of Law & Politics* 3, no. 1 (2010): 30–52.

Cherkaoui, Tarek. "Qatar's Public Diplomacy, International Broadcasting and the Gulf Crisis." *Rising Powers Quarterly* 3, no. 3 (2018): 129–149.

Chong, Alan. "Small State Soft Power Strategies: Virtual Enlargement in the Cases of the Vatican City State and Singapore." *Cambridge Review of International Affairs* 23, no. 3 (2010): 383–405.

Cooper, Andrew F. and Bessma Momani. "Qatar and Expanded Contours of Small State Diplomacy." *The International Spectator: Italian Journal of International Affairs* 46, no. 3 (2011): 113–128.

Cordina, Gordon. "Economic Resilience and Market Efficiency in Small States." In *Small States and the Pillars of Economic Resilience*, edited by L. Briguglio, G. Cordina, N. Farrugia and C. Vigilance. Valletta: Islands and Small States Institute, University of Malta, 2008.

Dahl, Robert A. "The Concept of Power." *Behavioral Science* 2, no. 3 (1957): 201–215.

David, Steven R. "Explaining Third World Alignment." *World Politics* 43, no. 2 (1991): 233–56.

De Gregori, Thomas R. "Resources Are Not; They Become: An Institutional Theory." *Journal of Economic Issues* XXI, no. 3 (1987): 1241–1263.

Deudney, Daniel H. "Environmental Security: A Critique." In *Contested Grounds: Security and Conflict in the New Environmental Politics*, edited by Daniel H. Deudney and Richard A. Matthew. Albany: State University of New York Press, 1999.

Doyle, Michael and Stefano Recchia. "Liberalism in International Relations." In *International Encyclopedia of Political Science*, edited by Bertrand Badie, Dirk-Berg Schlosser and Leonardo Morlina. Los Angeles: Sage, 2011.

Duffield, John S. "Alliances." In *Security Studies: An Introduction*, edited by Paul D. Williams and Matt McDonald, 267–281. London and New York: Routledge, 2018.

East, Maurice. "Size and Foreign Policy Behavior: A Test of Two Models." *World Politics* 25, no. 4 (1973): 556–576.

Easterly, William and Aart C. Kraay. "Small States, Small Problems? Income, Growth and Volatility in Small States." *World Development* 28, no. 11 (2002): 2013–2027.

Elman, Miriam Fendius. "The Foreign Policies of Small States: Challenging Neorealism in its Own Backyard." *British Journal of Political Science* 25, no. 2 (1995): 171–217.

Gebhard, Carmen. "Is Small Still Beautiful? The Case of Austria." *Swiss Political Science Review* 19, no. 3 (2013): 279–297.

Gigleux, Victor. "Explaining the Diversity of Small States' Foreign Policies through Role Theory." *Third World Thematics: A TWQ Journal* 1, no. 1 (2016): 27–45.

Good, Robert. "State-Building as Determinant of Foreign Policy in the New States." In *Neutralism and Non-Alignment: The New States* in World Affairs, edited by L. Martin, 3–12. New York: Praeger, 1962.

Graf, Andreas and David Lanz. "Switzerland as a Paradigmatic Case of Small-State Peace Policy?" *Swiss Political Science Review* 19, no. 3 (2013): 410–423.

Griffin, Thomas Ross. "National Identity, Social Legacy and Qatar 2022: The Cultural Ramifications of FIFA's First Arab World Cup." *Soccer and Society*, 20, no. 7–8 (2019): 1000–1013.

Grøn, Caroline Howard and Anders Wivel. "Maximizing Influence in the European Union After the Lisbon Treaty: From Small State Policy to Smart State Strategy." *Journal of European Integration* 33, no. 5 (2011): 523–539.

Guzansky, Yoel. "The Foreign-Policy Tools of Small Powers: Strategic Hedging in the Persian Gulf." *Middle East Policy* 22, no. 1 (Spring 2015): 112–122.

Hansen, P. "Adaptive Behavior of Small States: The Case of Denmark and the European Community." In *Sage International Yearbook of Foreign Policy Studies*, edited by J. McGowan, 143–174. London: Sage, 1974.

Harbert, J.R. "The Behavior of the Ministates in the United Nations, 1971-1972." *International Organization* 30, no.2 (1976): 109–127.

Harris, W.L. "Microstates in the United Nations: A Broader Purpose." *Columbia Journal of Transnational Law* 9 (1970): 23–53.

Hayter, Roger and Jerry Patchell "Resources Geography." In *International Encyclopedia of the Social & Behavioural Sciences*, 2nd edition, edited by James D. Wright, 568–575. Oxford: Elsevier, 2015.

Henrikson, A.K. "A coming 'Magnesian' Age? Small States, the Global System, and the International Community." *Geopolitics* 6, no. 2 (2001): 49–86.

Hong, M. "Small States in the United Nations." *International Social Science Journal* 47, no. 2 (1995): 77–287.

Ilyin, M. V. "Is a Universal Typology of States Possible?" *Political Science* 4, (2008): 8–41.

Ingebritsen, C. "Norm Entrepreneurs: Scandinavia's Role in World Politics." *Cooperation and Conflict* 37, no. 1 (2002): 11–23.

Jakobsen, Peter Viggo. "Small States, Big Influence: The Overlooked Nordic Influence on the Civilian ESDP." *Journal of Common Market Studies* 47, no. 1 (2009): 81–102.

Jervis, Robert. "Cooperation Under the Security Dilemma." *World Politics* 30, (1978): 167–214.

Katzenstein, Peter J. "The Smaller European States, Germany and Europe." In *Tamed Power: Germany in Europe*, edited by P. J. Katzenstein. Ithaca: Cornell University Press, 1997.

Kuznets, S. "Economic Growth of Small Nations." In *Economic Consequences of the Size of Nations*, edited by E. A. G. Robinson. New York: St. Martin's Press, 1960.

Keohane, Robert O. "Lilliputians' Dilemmas: Small States in International Politics." *International Organization* 23, no. 2 (Spring 1969): 291–310.

_____ "The Big Influence of Small Allies." *Foreign Policy* 2, (Spring 1971): 161–182.

Khatib, Lina. "Qatar's Foreign Policy: The Limits of Pragmatism." *International Affairs* 89, no. 2 (2013): 417–432.

Kingah, Stephen and Luk Van Langenhove. "Determinants of a Regional Organisation's Role in Peace and Security: The African Union and the European Union Compared." *South African Journal of International Affairs* 19, no. 2, (2012): 201–222.

Lamoreaux, Jeremy W. and David J. Galbreath. "The Baltic States As "Small States": Negotiating The "East" By Engaging The "West."" *Journal of Baltic Studies* 39, no. 1 (2008): 1–14.

Lee, Donna and Nicola J Smith. "Small State Discourses in the International Political Economy." *Third World Quarterly* 31, no. 7 (2010): 1091–1105.

Leeds, Brett, Jeffrey Ritter, Sara Mitchell and Andrew Long. "Alliance Treaty Obligations and Provisions, 1815–1944." *International Interactions* 28, no. 3 (2002): 237–260.

Legro, Jeffery W. and Andrew Moravcsik. "Is Anybody Still a Realist?" *International Security* 24, no. 2 (1999): 5–55.

Lobell, Steven, Neal Jesse and K. Williams. "Why Do Secondary States Choose to Support, Follow or Challenge?" *International Politics* 52, no. 2 (2015): 146–162.

Long, Tom. "Small States, Great Power? Gaining Influence Through Intrinsic, Derivative, and Collective Power." *International Studies Review* 19, no. 2 (2016): 185–205.

"It's Not Size, It's the Relationship: From 'Small States' to Asymmetry." *International Politics* 54, no. 2 (2017): 144–160.

Maass, Matthias. "The Elusive Definition of the Small State." *International Politics* 46, no. 1 (2009): 65–83.

_____ "Small Enough to Fail: The Structural Irrelevance of the Small State as Cause of its Elimination and Proliferation since Westphalia." *Cambridge Review of International Affairs* 29, no. 4 (2016): 1303–1323.

Magnusdottir, Gunnhirdur L. and Baldur Thorhallsson. "The Nordic States and Agenda-Setting in the European Union: How Do Small States Score?" *Stjornmal & Stjornsysla* 1, no. 7 (2011): 204–226.

Männik, E. "EU and the Aspirations of Applicant Small States: Estonia and the Evolving CESDP." *Current Politics and Economics of Europe* 11, no. 1 (2002): 77–90.

Maoz, Zeev. "Domestic Politics of Regional Security: Theoretical Perspectives and Middle East Patterns." *Journal of Strategic Studies* 26, no. 3 (2003): 9–48.

Mendelson, M. H. "Diminutive States in the United Nations." *International and Comparative Law Quarterly* 21 (1972): 609–630.

Miller, Rory. "Managing Regional Conflict: The Gulf Cooperation Council and the Embargo of Qatar." *Global Policy* 10, no. 2 (June 2019): 36–45.

―――― "Qatar, Energy Security, and Strategic Vision in a Small State." *Journal of Arabian Studies* 10, no. 1 (2020): 122–148.

Miller, Rory and Harry Verhoeven. "Overcoming Smallness: The UAE, Qatar and Strategic Realignment in the Gulf." *International Politics* 57, no. 1 (February 2020): 1–20.

Miller, Rory and Khalid Al-Mansouri. "Qatar's Foreign Policy Engagement with the European Union: Evolving Priorities of a Small State in the Contemporary Era." *Comillas Journal of International Relations* 5, (2016): 46–64.

Miller, Rory and Sarah Cardaun. "Multinational Security Coalitions and the Limits of Middle Power Activism in the Middle East: The Case of Saudi Arabia." *International Affairs* 96, no. 6 (November 2020): 1509–1529.

Mohammadzadeh, Babak. "Status and Foreign Policy Change in Small States: Qatar's Emergence in Perspective." *The International Spectator: Italian Journal of International Affairs* 52, no. 2 (2017): 19–36.

Mosser, Michael W. "Engineering Influence: The Subtle Power of Small States in the CSCE/OSCE." In *Small States and Alliances*, edited by E. Reiter and H. Gartner, 63–84. Leiden: Springer, 2001.

Mouritzen, Hans. "Small States and Finlandisation in the Age of Trump." *Survival* 59, no. 2 (2017): 67–84.

Panke, Diana. "Small States in EU Negotiations: Political Dwarfs or Power-Brokers?" *Cooperation and Conflict* 46, no.2 (2011): 123–143.

―――― "Dwarfs in International Negotiations: How Small States Make their Voices Heard." *Cambridge Review of International Affairs* 25, no. 3 (2012): 313–328.

―――― "Small States in Multilateral Negotiations. What Have We Learned?" *Cambridge Review of International Affairs* 25, no. 3 (September 2012): 387–398.

―――― "Studying Small States in International Security Affairs: A Quantitative Analysis." *Cambridge Review of International Affairs* 30, no. 2-3 (2017): 235–255.

Papadakis, M. and H. Starr. "Opportunity, Willingness, and Small States: The Relationship Between Environment and Foreign Policy." In *New Directions in the Study of Foreign Policy*, edited by C. F. Hermann, C. W. Kegley, J. Rosenau, 409–432. Boston: Allen & Unwin, 1987.

Payne, Anthony. "Small States in the Global Politics of Development." *The Round Table: The Commonwealth Journal of International Affairs* 93, no.376 (2004): 623–635.

Pfluke, Corey. "A History of the Five Eyes Alliance: Possibility for Reform and Additions." *Comparative Strategy* 38, no. 4 (2019): 302–315.

Quah, Jon S.T. "Why Singapore Works: Five Secrets of Singapore's Success." *Public Administration and Policy* 21, no. 1 (2018): 5–21.

Radoman, Jelena. "Small States in World Politics: State of the Art." *Journal of Regional Security* 13, no. 2 (2018): 179–200.

Rickli, Jean-Marc. "European Small States' Military Policies After the Cold War: From Territorial to Niche Strategies." *Cambridge Review of International Affairs* 21, no. 3 (September 2008): 307–325.

Ross, Ken. "The Commonwealth: A Leader For the World's States?" *The Round Table: The Commonwealth Journal of International* Affairs 86, no. 343 (1997): 411–419.

Rostoks, Tom. "Small States, Power, International Change and the Impact of Uncertainty." In *Small States in Europe: Challenges and Opportunities*, edited by Robert Steinmetz and Anders Wivel, 87–101. Farnham: Ashgate, 2010.

Schmitt, Olivier. "More Allies, Weaker Missions? How Junior Partners Contribute to Multinational Military Operations." *Contemporary Security Policy* 40, no. 1 (2019): 70–75.

Schweller, Randall L. "Bandwagoning for Profit: Bringing the Revisionist State Back In." *International Security* 19, no. 1 (1994): 72–107.

Sirimaneetham, Vatcharin and Jonathan R. W. Temple. "Macroeconomic Stability and the Distribution of Growth Rates." *World Bank Economic Review* 23, no. 3 (2009): 443–479.

Smirnov, Vadim. "The Role of Small Countries in Post-Soviet Territorial Restructuring: The Baltic Case." *Baltic Region* 4, no. 22 (2014): 42–49.

Sutton, Paul. "The Concept of Small States in the International Political Economy." *The Round Table: The Commonwealth Journal of International Affairs* 100, no. 413 (2011): 141–153.

Thorhallsson, Baldur. "Consequences of a Small Administration: The Case of Iceland." *Current Politics and Economics of Europe* 11, no. 1 (2002): 61–76.

———. "The Size of States in the European Union: Theoretical and Conceptual Perspectives." *Journal of European Integration* 28, no. 1 (2006): 7–31.

———. "Studying Small States: A Review." *Small States & Territories* 1, no. 1 (2018): 17–34.

Tokolyova, Tatiana. "Nation-Branding in Small-States Foreign Politics." *Journal of Geography, Politics and Society* 6, no. 4 (2016): 7–14.

Tonurist, Piret. "What Is a 'Small State' in a Globalising Economy?" *Halduskultuur – Administrative Culture* 11, no. 1 (2010): 8–29.

Tu'akoi, S., M. Vickers, K. Tairea, Y. Aung, N. Tamarua-Herman, M. 'Ofanoa and J. Bay. "The Significance of DOHaD for Small Island Developing States." *Journal of Developmental Origins of Health and Disease* 9, no. 5 (2018): 487–49.

Vaicekauskaite, Zivile Marija. "Security Strategies of Small States." *Journal of Baltic Security* 3, no. 2 (2017): 7–15.

Väyrynen, R. "On the Definition and Measurement of Small Power Status." *Cooperation and Conflict: Journal of the Nordic International Studies Association* 2, (1971): 91–102.

Veenendaal, Wouter P. "Analyzing the Foreign Policy of Microstates: The Relevance of the International Patron-Client Model." *Foreign Policy Analysis* 13, no.3 (2017): 561–577.

Von Däniken, Franz. "Is the Notion of Small State Still Relevant?" In *Small States Inside and Outside the European Union: Interests and Policies*, edited by L. Goetschel, 43–48. Boston, MA: Springer, 1998.

Wallander, Celeste A. "Institutional Assets and Adaptability: NATO After the Cold War." *International Organization* 54, no. 4 (Autumn 2000): 705–735.

Walt, Stephen M. "Alliance Formation and the Balance of World Power." *International Security* 9, no. 4 (1985): 3–43.

Wendt, Alexander. "Constructing International Politics." *International Security* 20, no. 1 (1995): 71–81.

Wiberg, Hakan. "Security Problems of Small Nations." In *Small States and the Security Challenge in the New Europe*, edited by Werner Bauwens, Armand Clesse and Olav Knudsen, 21–41. London: Brassey's, 1996.

Williams, Paul D. and Matt McDonald. "An Introduction to Security Studies." In *Security Studies: An Introduction*, edited by P. D. Williams and M. McDonald, 1–13. London and New York: Routledge, 2018.

Wirtz, James J. "A New Agenda for Security and Strategy?" In *Strategy in the Contemporary World*, 5th edition, edited by John Baylis et al., 337–354. Oxford: Oxford University Press, 2016.

Wivel, Anders. "The Security Challenge of Small EU Member States: Interests, Identity and the Development of the EU as a Security Actor." *Journal of Common Market Studies* 43, no. 2 (2005): 393–412.

———. "From Peacemaker to Warmonger? Explaining Denmark's Great Power Politics." *Swiss Political Science Review* 19, no. 3 (2013): 298–321.

Wivel, Anders and Kajsa Ji Noe Oest. "Security, Profit or Shadow of the Past? Explaining the Security Strategies of Microstates." *Cambridge Review of International Affairs* 23, no. 3 (2010): 429–453.

Wohlforth, William C., Benjamin de Carvalho, Halvard Leira and Iver B. Neumann. "Moral Authority and Status in International Relations: Good States and the Social Dimension of Status Seeking." *Review of International Studies* 44, no. 3 (2018): 526–546.

Wright, S. "Foreign Policies with International Reach: The Case of Qatar." In *The Transformation of the Gulf: Politics, Economics and the Global Order*, edited by David Held and Kristian Coates Ulrichsen. London: Routledge, 2011.